MW00815304

Stories from My Life

Cassandra Walker
Talks to Teens
about Growing Up

by Cassandra Walker

Edited by Elizabeth Verdick

Free Spirit® PUBLISHING

Library of Congress Cataloging-in-Publication Data

Walker, Cassandra, 1966–
     Stories from my life : Cassandra Walker talks to teens about
growing up / by Cassandra Walker.
         p.   cm.
     Summary: Stories from the author's life that deal with topics
related to growing up such as crushes, friends, family, divorce, and
self-esteem.
     ISBN 1-57542-016-3
     1. Walker, Cassandra, 1966– —Childhood and youth—
Juvenile literature. 2. Teenage girls—United States—Biography—
Juvenile literature. 3. Teenage girls—United States—Conduct of
life—Juvenile literature. [1. Walker, Cassandra, 1966– —Childhood
and youth. 2. Teenage girls. 3. Conduct of life.]
     I. Title.
HQ798.S554   1997
305.235—dc21   96–46698
                                                                              CIP
                                                                              AC

Cover design by Cindy Olson
Interior design by City Desktop Productions, Inc.

10 9 8 7 6 5 4 3 2 1

Printed in the United States of America

Free Spirit Publishing Inc.
400 First Avenue North, Suite 616
Minneapolis, MN 55401-1730
(612) 338-2068
help4kids@freespirit.com

I dedicate this book to my family: husband, Ron, and children, Shawn, Scott, Skyler, and Ron Jr. I also dedicate this book to my brother, Clinton Walker. It was because of you, Clinton, that I have so many memories and stories to write about.

Acknowledgments

Thank you, Dear Lord Jesus, for guiding me through another book that will help many young people.

Thank you, friends and family, for allowing me to tell your stories in such an honest and open manner.

A most special thank you to my wonderful, loving parents, Clinton A. and Odessa F. Walker, without whom none of this would be possible.

Thank you, Sayeh Nikpay and family, for your time and openness.

Thank you, Free Spirit staff, for all of your support and dedication to my book.

Contents

Introduction

"No matter how small your talent
or opportunity may seem to you,
make the best of it!"

Ronald K. Suggs, Sr.

When I was a young girl growing up in Chicago, I never thought that all of my growing pains would inspire not one, but two, books for young people. I was so overwhelmed by the response from readers of my first book, *Becoming Myself*, that I was prompted to write another book—this one.

My success is a confirmation of what the Pulitzer-Prize winning author, Alex Haley, who wrote the best-seller *Roots* (about his African-American heritage), once told me when I had the chance to meet him in my early twenties. He said that everyone has a gift, and while your particular talent may not seem like much to you, you must nurture it and work hard to help it grow. His encouraging words were an inspiration to me. I realized that all of us, no matter how or where we grow up, are capable of making the most of our gift and sharing it with others.

Over the years, I've told my story in the hopes that I might help children and teens who are feeling the self-doubt I often felt while growing up. In response, I've been fortunate to receive letters from people all around the world. Now I know for certain that growing up is just as difficult for a young person in America as it is for those who live elsewhere. We all have the same hurts and hopes, and the desire to one day get through it all and stay happy.

I've learned that divorce, death, poverty, joy, loneliness, despair, fear, happiness, struggles, and fulfillment span the globe to touch every girl and boy, man and woman. While growing up, we all experience changes and challenges that help us to become the special person we're striving to be.

I believe that each of you, no matter who you are or where you live, can and will become an important person in our society. You may think that your talents or gifts are small, but you can work hard to nurture them. You will achieve success if you believe in yourself, strive for the best, and never give up.

In this book, you'll read how I made countless mistakes and how I, like you, felt that I would never get beyond them. But with God's direction, and through perseverance, I have survived. I'm still surviving, and I know that you will, too. You'll also read about the experiences of my friends and family, and how the many people I've known throughout my life have influenced me and helped me to grow. Through them, I learned many valuable lessons about life—lessons that continue to help me learn and grow, even though I'm now an adult and have children of my own.

Keep reaching for the stars, and don't let anyone tell you that you can't make it. If they tell you otherwise, know that you have at least one person believing in you—and that's me. If you're not getting the encouragement you need, or if you have growing-up problems that you can't talk about with someone you know, write to me. I'll write back to you, and together we can figure out how you can get through the bad times and keep reaching. Other young people have written to me in the past, and some of their letters are reprinted in this book (see pages 117–151). I hope that reading about their struggles will help you to see that growing up is a challenge for so many of us. You're not alone!

Write to me in care of:

Free Spirit Publishing Inc.
400 First Avenue North, Suite 616
Minneapolis, MN 55401-1730

Or contact me by email:

help4kids@freespirit.com

I invite you to recite this poem and keep it in your heart:

When I look in the mirror,
I see someone looking back at me.
Sometimes I'm not happy with who I see.
But the face staring back will always be me.
So I will strive to be the best I can be,
Because if I do, I'll see
A world of opportunity just waiting for me.

Stay in touch. And always remember these words that have helped me (perhaps they can help you, too): *The only thing between you and esteem is self.*

Cassandra Walker

1

Crushes

"Love yourself first and everything else falls in line."

Lucille Ball

He's a Thriller

I'm not exactly sure when it was that I first saw him, or even when I first heard him sing. But one thing is for sure: By the time I reached my junior year in high school, I was deeply in love with singer/superstar Michael Jackson.

I'd had a secret crush on him since I was a little girl. My love for Michael started to escalate in junior high when he went solo with his *Off the Wall* album. At that time, I just thought I was like any other preteen girl who admired Michael and his talent. But I wasn't. My crush continued to grow and grow.

By eleventh grade, my emotions were spinning out of control. Now, I had heard of teen idol crushes, and I was aware that lots of young people had them. But my situation was different. I truly believed I would one day marry Michael.

What started out as a harmless crush had turned into an obsession. My whole life centered around Michael Jackson. When I woke up in the morning, I played one of his songs, kissed ten of my almost fifty posters of him on my wall, then went to my bathroom to see even more posters of Michael. I would get dressed and put on two or three of my Michael Jackson buttons, grab my textbooks that had Michael book covers, snatch up my Michael Jackson key chain, and head off to school to talk about who else but . . . Michael? I even had "I love Michael Jackson" shoelaces. Yeah, I was totally out there.

Before I knew it, I found that I was more concerned about what Michael was doing than what I was doing. I stopped studying to daydream about Michael. I was so wrapped up with Michael Jackson and *his* life that I put my own life on hold. I stopped studying, and my grades started to drop. I wrote more letters to Michael than I did English assignments.

My friends and relatives tried to tell me to cool it, but I just figured they were jealous because I was going to be "Mrs. Michael Jackson." If someone had a Michael poster or button that I didn't have, I would become very upset. On the outside, I tried to make it seem as if I just liked him a little and that my crush was no big deal. But inside, I was dying to meet him at all costs.

The spring of my junior year, I received my midterm grades. I was usually a good student with a B average, but this time I opened my report card to find three F's. "How could this be?" I thought. "I usually breeze through these classes. My parents are going to kill me!"

Although they didn't kill me, they left a lasting impression: I was informed "NO MORE MICHAEL!" until my grades improved. My parents then took away every poster, button, shoelace, teen book, album, or anything else that had to do with Michael Jackson. The worst part was when my mom and dad said that I couldn't write letters to Michael anymore. I thought the world had just ended.

Believe it or not, I survived the next three months without Michael Jackson. But it wasn't easy! I soon found other things to do, instead of drooling over my idol. I read my textbooks, and my grades improved. I learned about the world and all that's in it (other than Michael). I also worked on getting myself ready for track season. Gradually, I started to see that Michael Jackson was a person, not a god. I found a new world out there, and it made me see just how far I'd slipped from the real one.

Even today, I sometimes look back on how obsessed I was with Michael Jackson. But now I just admire him from afar and wish him well, especially considering that he's had his share of troubles. Besides, I don't know if I could have gotten used to the name Cassandra Jackson.

I know it's fun to have crushes on celebrities and to daydream about them. But if you find that your life is going downhill and your every waking thought is about that superstar (or anyone else, for that matter), it's time to take a good, hard look at yourself. Are you forgetting to study, to try new hobbies, to spend time with your friends and family? There are so many things in life that you can be interested in, learn about, and try. Crushes are normal, but don't let your life get crushed in the process.

Be Careful Who You Fall in Love with

In seventh grade, it seemed like everyone in my class was starting to get interested in the opposite sex. For the first time, I started liking guys who were a lot older than me—guys like my substitute math teacher, Mr. Kubel.

Our previous math teacher had left the school about two months into the school year. Mr. Kubel was hired as a temporary replacement. At first, I thought that Mr. Kubel was just a cute young man. Soon I started daydreaming about him, and then I realized I had a serious crush on him. I was always eager to answer any math problems that he wrote on the board. I was the first one to arrive in class and the last one to leave. I had it bad for Mr. Kubel.

After class one day, I was talking with Mr. Kubel, and we learned that we lived near each other. Turns out, he lived only about two blocks away from my family. I told him that if there was ever anything he needed, he should be sure and let me know, seeing as we were neighbors. Mr. Kubel treated me so nicely, and he always had time for me. I convinced myself that he liked me just as much as I liked him, even though there was an eleven-year age difference between us.

One day, I worked up the nerve to walk by Mr. Kubel's house. He said I could stop by anytime, and since I knew he was single, I figured I wouldn't be intruding on any family time. I remember walking up to the door and ringing the doorbell. I was so nervous. Mr. Kubel answered with his friendly grin and greeted me with a big hello.

He invited me in, saying he was just talking about me and how I was one of his favorite students. "I *knew* he liked me," I thought to myself. Then Mr. Kubel said he wanted me to meet someone special to him. I remember thinking, "Oh, boy, he already wants me to meet his mother—I hope she likes me."

Well, the "someone" wasn't his mother, although she *was* female. I don't remember her name, but she told me she was Mr. Kubel's fiancée. They said they were getting married soon. I couldn't move a muscle. I just stood there and stared. Somehow, I got out of that house, and I ran all the way home crying. "How could I have been so stupid?" I thought.

For the next few weeks, math class was terrible for me. I didn't participate like I used to. I was the last one to arrive in class and the first one to leave. Mr. Kubel often questioned me about my sudden change in behavior, but I just shrugged my shoulders.

One morning, I entered the classroom and was surprised to find that Mr. Kubel wasn't there. A heavy-set man in his late forties stood by the blackboard. "I'm going to be your math teacher for the rest of the school year," he said to the class. The new teacher then told us that Mr. Kubel had found a permanent position at another school. I felt terrible that Mr. Kubel was gone and that I had never explained my true feelings or my behavior. I still sometimes think about Mr. Kubel and wonder if he has ever thought about me over the years.

A teacher is there to guide you and to help you grow. You can admire your teacher, but convincing yourself that you're in love only takes you away from the real reason you're at school: to learn. Stay focused on your school work—that's really the best way to get your teacher's attention.

To Date or Not to Date (That Is the Question)

Wow, I was finally sixteen years old. This was quite a milestone for me. My parents had always told me that at sixteen I could officially start dating. Well, now was my big chance. "Watch out, all you eligible young men," I told myself.

Ever since I could remember, I'd been wondering what it was like to go on a date. On television, dating always seemed so fun. The guy would pick the girl up, and they would go to the movies or out to eat. To me, dating seemed like pretending to be an adult.

For some reason, I assumed that when I turned sixteen all the boys would know I was ready to date. I figured they'd be knocking down my door, begging me to go out with them. Well, the telephone wires must have been down because no boys were calling me! At first, this didn't bother me too much because some of my close friends weren't dating, either.

My friends and I started to get used to not being invited to the various high school dances that came and went. By my senior year, I *still* hadn't gone on an official date. I had a boyfriend (Ron) for a couple months during my junior year, but the two of us never went out anywhere special. We mainly studied together or spent time with each other at school. I still was waiting for a boy to take me to dinner, a dance, or a movie. Only one other friend of mine was in the same situation.

Then it happened—the day I knew would come. You guessed it: My friend was asked to go on a date and I wasn't. So there I was, the only one in my circle of friends who had never been asked for a date. I was humiliated. I felt like something must be wrong with me.

Somehow, the boys I knew just didn't see me as date material. They thought I was nice, and I had a lot of guy friends—but still no dates. I pretended like it didn't bother me, and I told everyone that I was too busy for dating anyway. The truth is, I was at home watching television every Friday or Saturday night. I wasn't busy at all.

One day, a close friend of mine named Jerry asked me to join him and a few other guys and girls who were going to the movies. So I went. We hung out as a group of friends and had a great time. No one felt pressured to pair off or to act like we were on dates. Then it hit me: This was a great way to be with other people, to be a part of a group, and to have fun. No more weekends alone at home in front of the TV!

I learned that it was okay to invite a group of friends over for pizza at my house or to go to a movie together. From then on, every weekend I would have a "date"—

with a group of people I enjoyed spending time with. I did find out later in life that one-on-one dating is fun. Meanwhile, I was enjoying the comfort of having a lot of friends and good times.

Dating and being in a relationship may seem so important when you're in high school. But there are lots of other things you can do, such as concentrate on your studies, participate in sports, be in a play, hang out with your friends, and simply enjoy your free time. If you're not dating, try not to waste your energy feeling lonely or left out. Instead, work on making some close friends and including new people in your weekend activities. Throw a small party, invite friends over for pizza or videos, and make plans for group "dates" where everyone can join in and feel as if they're part of the crowd.

Is This Love?

I was seventeen when I first noticed him: Mr. Tall, Dark, and Handsome. His name was Ron Suggs. Ron was seventeen, too, and he was new to our high school. My friends said Ron was very kind, outgoing—and TAKEN! Woe was me! I tried not to fall for Ron, but I couldn't help myself. It was torture seeing him with, you know . . . *the other woman.*

I admired Ron from afar but didn't tell him I liked him. I let my friends know about my heartfelt dilemma, and they all told me the same thing: "He already has a girlfriend." Of course, I knew that bit of helpful information (leave it to your friends to rub it in once in a while—after all, what are friends for?).

My crush on Ron grew bigger each day, and soon all I ever thought about was him. Then one day, I heard that Ron had broken up with "the other woman," and to me, this was great news. I won't say exactly how excited I was, but I did three cartwheels and a back walkover in the school parking lot. Of course, I had to try to get control of myself—after all, this was a sad thing, the breakup of a romance. (Who am I trying to fool? I was elated!)

Now I had to figure out how to get Ron to notice me. I contemplated this for days, wondering if I should try the sympathy approach ("Oh, Ron, I heard about your recent breakup, I'm so sorry . . . are you available next Saturday?"). I decided that tactic would be too forward. I wondered if I should bump into him on purpose and see if he would pick up my books, giving me the chance to strike up a conversation. No—I remembered I had tried that method once, and the guy I liked simply stepped on my books and kept on walking. With Ron, I decided to just be myself. Uh-oh!

Actually, it wasn't as hard as I'd expected. Ronnie (as I came to call him) and I gradually became friends and started hanging out with the same group of people. One day, he asked the big question: Would I be his girl-friend? I eagerly said yes.

We began to spend a lot of time together. At school, Ronnie walked me to every class and carried my books. He met me before and after my cheerleading and track practices. At night, we talked on the phone. Yes, we were in L-O-V-E.

After two or three months of this, some of my friends started saying that Ronnie was smothering me and taking up too much of my time. They said it was unhealthy for him to always want to be around me. I started to take these remarks seriously. Soon I was falling out of love with Ronnie. I didn't want him to walk me to my classes, and I tried to avoid him when he stopped by my locker. The more I thought about what my friends were saying, the more I believed they were right.

Finally, Ronnie started to notice this change in me, and he asked me if I wanted to break up. I said yes. I didn't know it then, but I really hurt him. Time went on, and we didn't speak to each other. I never offered him an explanation; I just turned away whenever I saw him.

We graduated and went our separate ways, and over the next ten years or so, I lost track of Ronnie. But after a while, I wanted to apologize for how I had acted. I tried to find him by contacting his family, but they had moved away. I was too late.

I realized the hurt and pain I must have caused Ronnie, and I was truly sorry. I eventually got the chance to apologize at our ten-year high school reunion. As soon as I saw Ronnie, I gave him a hug and told him how sorry I was. He accepted my apology, and our relationship was mended.

I'm happy to say that a year after we were reunited, we decided to make a lifelong commitment to each other, and we got married. Although I once hurt Ronnie deeply, I will now love him for a lifetime.

It can be fun to date in high school, but it's okay to take each relationship slowly. You don't have to spend every moment together to show how serious you are. Above all, treat the person you're dating with care because you're dealing with someone's emotions. It's better to be honest about your feelings and needs than to hurt someone by just turning away. Maybe the two of you can arrive at a solution together. Always treat your special person with the same love and respect that you want for yourself.

Pucker Up

I t starts as something you're embarrassed about when your parents or grandparents do it to you in public. Then it becomes something you're very curious about when you're a preteen or teen. Of course, I'm talking about KISSING. Suddenly, you hit an age where you spend a lot of time wondering what it's like to be kissed by someone you have a crush on.

I didn't really think about kissing all that much unless I saw it on television. On TV, kissing seemed fun and romantic and fairytale-like. This kind of kissing wasn't at all like the quick pecks on the cheeks that my parents would give each other as they headed off to work each morning.

When I was thirteen, it seemed that all of my friends had gotten their first real kiss already. I don't mean a peck from a curious neighbor boy or some young cousin who didn't know you were related. (Those were the only kisses I had experienced from a boy.) I'm talking about *real* kisses—the kind where you hold your lips together longer than it takes to blink, the kind of kisses that could be seen on TV and in the movies.

Now, don't get me wrong. I was no stranger to how kissing actually worked. I had practiced many times on my bedroom mirror, and I had become quite a pro. I was convinced that when I finally found a boyfriend, I would get at least a B on my first real kiss.

Some may call me innocent, and others may say that I was right on course, but I didn't get my first real kiss until I was seventeen. That's because I didn't have a real boyfriend (Ron) until that time. I wasn't in any big hurry to kiss him, but my friends kept asking me if we had kissed yet. Every time they asked this, I felt more and more pressured.

One of my girlfriends had even graduated from kissing with just her lips—she was into French kissing, with an open mouth. "Yuck, who would want to do that?" I asked her, to which she replied, "The French."

But it eventually happened: I got my first kiss. I remember it like it was yesterday. I was cheerleading at a basketball game, and Ronnie (as I called him) was on the team. After the game, we were talking and he gave me a hug. Then, just as if it were the most natural thing in the world, Ronnie leaned toward me and we kissed. It was very strange at first—not at all like kissing my bedroom mirror. I'm sure the kiss lasted no longer than a few seconds, but it felt like an hour. Then it was over. That was it.

The next day, I told my friends, and they were so excited. But I was thinking to myself that I had waited seventeen years for that kiss, and when it finally happened I didn't see any firecrackers or shooting stars. As I got older, I learned that kissing gets better with age and maturity. That's because you get a little more practice (on real people). And when you're really in love with someone, kissing means a lot more to both of you and is more special.

Are you still waiting for your first real kiss? Don't rush the experience. And don't expect your first kiss to bring shooting stars or a bright, glorious glow to your face. The first kiss is special, and you'll probably remember it for the rest of your life. But it's also worth waiting for. Make sure you're really ready for it, instead of letting other people pressure you into moving faster than you want to. The most important thing I want to tell you about kissing is that it's okay to stop there and leave the rest until later (as in when you get married).

2

Lessons from Life

"Though life's road will twist and turn, we must not become discouraged."

Booker T. Washington

Watch Your Mouth!

Why is it that young people often love to do the very things they aren't supposed to do, especially when no adults are around to catch them in the act? I have to admit that when I was younger, I did and said things that my parents had told me not to. I remember one particular incident that involved cursing.

Now, I'm sure you know all about curse words and swearing, and that you've tried out a few of those forbidden words a few or more times. When I was growing up, things were a little more strict. You didn't hear people swearing as much on TV and in movies. In my family, people simply didn't curse. So, I never really felt the need to either.

That is, I never wanted to swear until I met a new friend in junior high who could curse like a pro. And her best friend was the same way. Somehow, they chose me as the person they wanted to walk to school with. I was curious about these two girls because they seemed more grown-up and worldly than I was. So, I walked with them to school each day, trying not to cringe every time the F-word popped out of their mouths.

As the days turned to weeks, I got used to the swearing. It seemed natural and cool to curse. Their tough vocabulary seemed very adult (even though the adults in my life certainly wouldn't have approved). Soon the cool guys in school were hanging around the three of us. I was feeling cooler by the minute.

One day, as we were walking home from school, I dropped my books and much to my surprise yelled out, "#!*#" Everyone around me stopped, looked at me with astonishment, and said, "Oooooh." Then I realized that my next-door neighbor's mother was right there, giving me a look that only a mother could give. I tried to convince her that I usually didn't use such unthinkable words. But she'd heard the way the word had rolled off my tongue so smoothly, and she wasn't the least bit convinced.

Now, this may not seem like a big deal, but believe me, it was. I knew I could get into trouble for swearing, and I dreaded the moment my mother returned from work to hear the whole story. My neighbor's mom was ready to tell it all. The two of us were waiting on the front porch when my mom arrived.

My mother listened to the report with a scowl on her face. By the time the story was finished, I was tried, convicted, and on my way to jail (or so it seemed). My mom said she planned to tell my dad, and that the two of them would have to think of a proper punishment. They made me apologize to our neighbor's mom and said I couldn't use the phone for two weeks.

When I went back to school the next day, I told another friend of mine about what had happened. She said, "So, you finally got caught cursing." I was surprised at her remark. I told her that it was the first time I'd ever sworn and that I was unlucky enough to get caught. My friend then said something that really made me wake up: "Cassandra, ever since you've been hanging around those girls, everyone just assumed you talked the same way they do."

I was shocked because I had never realized that people might judge me for who I hung around with, rather than for who I was. It hadn't occurred to me that the behavior of my new friends might reflect on me, or even rub off on me.

After that incident, I slowly started to move away from those two girls. I had come to realize that I really was acting like them, and that I no longer felt like myself. Somewhere along the way, I'd forgotten my values and the values of my family. It was hard to leave my new friends behind, but I was determined not to lose my own identity.

When you're choosing your friends or a group to hang out with, be aware of who you pick and why. If you decide to spend time with people who seem cooler, more grown up, or tougher than you, you're probably not making the choice that's right for you. Take another look at yourself: Are you happy with the person you are now or the person you're becoming?

I found out the hard way that friends can either make you or break you. Things could have been worse, though: My new friends could have been into drugs or other, riskier behaviors, and I might have done worse things than swearing. Look for friends who share your values, beliefs, and goals. Find people who can support you, encourage you, and lift you up when you need it.

Where Did You Get Those Bruises?

One of my close friends, Monique, lived in another neighborhood, and we spent a lot of time with each other. We often got together with the kids in her neighborhood to play tag and tug-of-war, and to hold races in the middle of the street. I remember running around until it got dark, and hearing her mother call for us to come home.

All of the kids in her neighborhood were fun to be around, and I got to know them well. But one boy in the group was very hard to reach. He joined in the games but seemed distant. His name was Manuel, and he always wore long-sleeved shirts. He didn't talk much. I never thought he was strange, just shy.

Once, during a game of outdoor hide-and-seek, my friend and I hid near an older-looking home surrounded by a big fence. As we knelt down in the grass to keep out of sight, we heard screaming and hitting sounds coming from inside the house. A kid's voice yelled, "Stop! Don't hit me anymore. Please!" Monique and I became afraid and ran back to her house.

That night, we talked about what we'd heard and wondered who lived in the house with the fence. But soon we were discussing the block party that would be held in her neighborhood in a few days. We quickly forgot about the yelling and hitting, and we didn't tell our parents.

At the block party, the sun was shining brightly and we were all feeling hot. One boy's parents brought out a hose for fun and started to spray us to cool us down. Everyone got really wet. Manuel was soaked from head to toe, and he decided to take off his shirt. All of us just stood and stared. The boy had large, blue bruises covering his arms and back. When he realized everyone was looking at him with alarmed expressions, he quickly ran home. Monique and I followed him and discovered that he lived at the house with the fence.

That's when we realized what was really going on. It all added up: the bruises, the yelling and hitting, the long-sleeved shirts that covered up the marks. Manuel was being abused at home.

I didn't know what to do or whether I should tell anyone what we'd learned. But soon enough, all of the kids in Monique's neighborhood knew the story. No one did anything about the situation, though. Instead of telling an adult we could trust, we ignored the abuse and pretended it didn't exist. I think we all just felt powerless. Now, when I look back, I regret we didn't do something to help that boy.

If you know someone who is being abused, or even if you just suspect abuse, tell an adult you trust and *don't put it off*. You could end up saving someone's life. If you are the one who is being abused, you can find help. Tell a trusted adult such as a teacher, clergy member, counselor, doctor, or someone else you can confide in. He or she will help you to know the truth—that the abuse isn't your fault, and you don't deserve it.

Lies, Lies, Lies

Sometimes it seems easier to tell a lie than to tell the truth and risk getting into trouble. At least, that's the way I figured it when I was growing up.

Long ago, when I was just a kid, I realized that twisting the truth was a way to get myself off the hook. For example, when my mom asked me who had messed up my room, I would answer that a big monster had done it. She would look at me and say, "Well, you clean it up, and if I see that monster, I'll deal with him." I was surprised when she fell for my story, but now I know she was just humoring me.

As I got older, my lies became more believable. You know how it goes: Little lies become big lies, which become bigger lies, and so on. Soon you hear yourself saying things like: "I never told your secret. . . . I aced the test, even though I didn't study. . . . Me, skip class?—never. . . . I didn't cheat. . . . I'm too sick to go to school today. . . ," etc. Later on in your life, the lies you tell can become even more complicated. You might find yourself lying about how a boyfriend *really* treats you, or sneaking in to work late but telling your boss that you're always on time. You may even find that you're lying to yourself.

In my own life, I told lies and then had to tell more lies to keep up with the lies I had told before. No one seemed to catch on that I was lying. It was hard for me to remember who I had lied to, and when, and why I had told the lie in the first place. I spent a lot of time just trying to cover my tracks. After a while, the lies and the truth became blurred. I found it very hard to live with the lies. I finally realized that I was not only hurting the people I was lying to, but also myself.

As an adult, I still get the urge to lie every once in a while. Sometimes it's just plain hard to tell the truth, especially if the truth could hurt someone you care about. But as the old saying goes: "Honesty is the best policy." That may seem trite, but I've found that most of the time the saying holds true.

Fighting Prejudice

When I was ten, I asked my mother if she had ever experienced prejudice. I recall what she said, and it had a powerful effect on me. This is her story, as she told it to me.

I had not felt the pain of racism, being sheltered by my father who was a very respected minister. But when I left home to go to nursing school, I got my first taste of prejudice.

We were separated into a black class and a white class, with all of us sharing the same classroom and teacher. I was expected to sit in the back row because I was black. The white students got to sit at the front of the class. They were called "Miss," while the black students were just referred to as "Nurse." I endured this discrimination because I desperately wanted to become a nurse.

After being in school one year, we were all needed to work as staff nurses, under the supervision of registered nurses, at Grady Memorial Hospital in Atlanta, Georgia. The black nurses got together, and we decided we didn't want to be referred to as "Nurse" anymore. To make our position known, we held a sit-in—an organized protest. All of the black nurses, nursing students, graduates, and supervisors met in the auditorium. We notified the nursing director that we wouldn't accept being called "Nurse," unless all of the nurses, black and white, were called "Nurse."

The nursing director was stunned. She told us to go back to work because our patients needed us. But we did not move. We were determined to hold our ground. The director then promised to call an administrative meeting to discuss our request at a later date. Still we did not move.

We had decided that we would all stick together, no matter how much we wanted to go back to our patients. So we did not move. Finally, in desperation, the nursing director told us (in a not-so-nice tone): "Put tape over your name badges, and write 'Miss' on them. Then go back to work." And we did.

Our sit-in changed things. The black nurses never again responded when called "Nurse." All of the students, black and white, were now referred to as "Miss."

My mother told me never to think negative thoughts about myself, or let someone treat me badly because of my race or any other part of me that could be perceived as "different." I'm telling you the same thing. If you feel you are being discriminated against for any reason, take a stand. Stick up for yourself, report the discriminator, or hold a nonviolent protest like my mother did. Violence is never a solution. Use your mind, not your fists.

3

Family Time

"It's not the amount of people,
but the amount of love, that
makes a family."

Cassandra Walker

Vacations

I remember getting so excited about going on family vacations. We would drive for eighteen hours to visit my grandmother in Virginia Beach, Virginia. The car ride always held fun and adventure. We would take board games, plenty of food and beverages, pillows, and blankets. I looked forward to lots of conversation during the drive.

The car trip was always fun until my brother, Clint, and I had endured all we could of the closeness a backseat could bring. Then the conversation would take a turn for the worse, and the fighting would start: "Move over," "You're squeezing me," "Your feet stink," "You're using up all the air." The backseat soon became a war zone. I realized that our family vacations meant happiness and horror all rolled into one.

Our mother would tell us to stop arguing and to enjoy each other, and our father would say that traveling as a family was a way to become closer. They insisted that we'd someday look back on these times with a smile. When Clint and I were fighting, I thought that the only thing that would truly make me smile would be "accidentally" leaving my brother at one of those delightful rest stops we frequented. Now, *that* would bring a *huge* smile to my face.

I must admit that, on these vacations, I enjoyed having my brother around to discuss the sights. When we stopped at a hotel, it was fun swimming and going to the arcade with Clint. But at the hotel, we had to share a bed, and with all that pushing and shoving and blanket snatching, all I wanted to do was smother Clint with my pillow in the middle of the night.

When we finally got to Grandma's, my brother and I would spend hours walking up and down the road, seeing the sights. At the beach, we'd see who could find the biggest and prettiest seashell; the loser had to buy the winner a candy apple. At night, we'd lie in our beds, talking about what we'd done that day and how much fun we'd had. Then, before we knew it, our parents would tell us it was time to make the return trip home. Once again, Clint and I would start quarreling in the backseat. By the time we got home, we'd be enemies again.

When my brother turned seventeen, he asked my parents if he could stay home instead of going on the family vacation that year. He decided that he was getting too old for the trip and wouldn't enjoy himself anymore. After some thought, my parents agreed to let him stay home. Wow, I was thrilled to death! I would have the backseat all to myself, and I wouldn't have to share a bed at the hotel. No more stinky feet in the car, and no more arguing. I was looking forward to this trip, for sure.

When vacation time arrived, we headed off and the ride was so pleasant. I looked out the window at the scenery and told my parents about everything I saw. But soon they started discussing the route we were taking, and they couldn't participate in my sightseeing anymore. "Oh, well," I thought, "I can play a game." Unfortunately, all of the games I knew were for two or more people. So I just looked forward to arriving at the hotel, where I knew I'd have a blast.

I went swimming in the hotel pool, but after an hour or so, I was bored and went back to our room. I figured the trip would improve once we reached my grandmother's house. But at her house, I was still bored. I actually found myself wishing that my brother had come along. Nothing was the same. I didn't even buy a candy apple.

I realized something on the car trip home to Illinois: Family vacations do make you closer. But you may not be aware of it until the day you're no longer taking those vacations. My brother and I had grown up and grown closer together during those days of sitting in the back-seat of the car, suffering through stinky socks and the summer heat. On that long trip home, I understood how much Clint and my family meant to me.

Enjoy your family vacations, no matter how uncomfortable things seem to get. Believe it or not, sometimes a little discomfort can bring lots of joy and fond memories. One day, you'll look back and smile at the times your family spent together. I know I did.

New People and Places

When I was younger, I thought it would be great to travel all over the world and to live in different places. But my family lived in only two neighborhoods over the years. Sometimes I felt I didn't have enough opportunities for exploring exotic places, and I dreamed of moving to foreign lands.

My three cousins—Angie, Candy, and Cecelia—had the kinds of opportunities that I could only dream of. Their father (my Uncle Aaron) was in the air force, and he was often stationed all over the country, and even overseas. I loved it when my cousins told me about the various places they had lived, and I thought it was cool that they were each born in different states.

My cousins got to experience so many new things. I tried to learn more about the world through their stories and memories. When they lived in London, England, I thought about how it was nighttime there when it was daytime where I lived. I found books about England so I could picture where my cousins had their home.

I also enjoyed visiting my cousins' family when I had the chance. Aunt Vonnie let us stay up late, and we would sing and dance and tell stories until we fell asleep. I remember one time when I went to their house in

Alabama that was situated on an air force base. When we drove up to the base, the guards at the entrance saluted because Uncle Aaron was a colonel and they could tell by the sticker on the family's car. I felt special and very proud to be a part of this.

I really admired and envied the life my cousins lived. I thought my life seemed boring in comparison. But one day, my cousin Candy told me that living all over the world wasn't as exciting as I thought it was. Sure, she enjoyed traveling and seeing new places, but there were disadvantages, too. Candy said that moving around all the time meant learning to find her way around a new community or city, getting used to a new house, and making new friends all the time. It also meant leaving behind old friends and boyfriends.

Candy told me about how she'd had three different orthodontists over the years and had to wear her braces longer than planned because her family moved around so much. (I understood how bad she felt about that, because I also had to wear braces, and I counted the days until they came off!) And when she learned how to drive, Candy had to figure out how to navigate the highways and roads in the new cities her family lived in.

Whenever the air force reassigned Uncle Aaron, his family had to leave familiar places and people behind. Candy explained to me that when it came time to go to her high school reunion, she didn't go because she didn't feel close to her classmates. She had attended more than one high school over the years and wasn't really attached to any of them.

I understood what Candy meant by the challenges of living in so many places. It would be hard to go to unfamiliar areas and meet new people constantly. Still, a part of me thinks it also must have been a wonderful series of adventures.

If your family has to move a lot, hang in there. Putting down roots in a new place can be difficult, but it can also be terrific. You'll meet new people, see new places, and have a wealth of experiences that most people can only imagine. Life always brings change. As you learn to adjust and bounce back, you'll end up stronger and better prepared for the next challenge.

Divorce

To me, "family" always meant stability, a home, a sense of belonging. When I was young, I also thought family meant a mother, a father, and children. But as I got older, I realized that families, like people, come in all different sizes and types.

My friend Carol and I were very close when we were in grade school. We often spent time together at each other's homes. Her dad, who was a police officer, was very funny and handsome. At sleepovers, he played games with us and kept us entertained.

I remember one day when Carol told me a secret about her family. She said that her mom and dad were getting a divorce. I immediately felt sorry for Carol. How could her family break up that way?

"Which of your parents will be leaving?" I asked her. She replied, "My dad."

I was hurt, and I would miss her dad. But I knew Carol would miss him even more. Someone she loved and was very close to wouldn't be a part of her everyday life anymore. Carol and her father would now have to schedule their visits and plan the time they could spend together. The divorce was very hard on Carol, and she had a tough time dealing with it all. She transferred to another school and had to adjust to a different life.

This happened in the 1970s, when divorce wasn't as common as it is today. At the time, I really started thinking about what a family is and how much my own family meant to me. Over the years, I saw other people I knew go through divorce, and each time it was a difficult process. I came to understand that families don't always have a mother, a father, and children living together in the same home—but this doesn't mean they aren't a family.

Today, there are all kinds of families. Maybe you live with your mom and dad, like I did. Or, maybe you have a single parent, a foster family, an adoptive family, or are being raised by your grandparents. Whatever your situation, you're still a family and you can still be close.

If your parents are divorced or are going through a divorce, it's important to know that the divorce isn't your fault. Sometimes young people blame themselves in this type of situation, but they shouldn't. Divorce is hard on everyone involved; it may feel like your world is falling apart. In time, I know you will adjust to the changes.

Bible School

My brother and I were raised in a Christian home, and we attended church regularly. At church, we had a lot of friends, and we enjoyed talking about Jesus with them. But in our neighborhood, we had a different set of friends. We rarely mentioned church or Jesus to them.

My mother was very religious, and one summer she decided to hold a vacation Bible school in our backyard. This meant that kids from the neighborhood would come over for two hours a day for one whole week to learn about Jesus. My mother asked my brother, Clint, and I to find kids in the neighborhood who might be interested in participating. We didn't want to do this, and we felt uncomfortable approaching our neighborhood friends.

Clint and I felt that talking about God to our church friends was okay, because they were part of the same religion and they already knew about Him. But with our other friends, talking about religion seemed difficult, and we were afraid they'd laugh at us. I felt embarrassed, and I thought my neighborhood friends might think my family was different.

But Clint and I did what our mother asked. We told our neighborhood friends about the Bible school, and some of them laughed at us. When it was time for Bible school to start, we were sure that no one would show up. That morning, my mother set up chairs and a portable chalkboard in our garage. On every chair was a Bible and some paper and pencils. Clint and I looked at each other uncomfortably, figuring all this effort was going to be for nothing.

We couldn't believe it when the first two kids showed up. Our close friends David and Terri, from across the street, arrived in our garage and sat down in two of the chairs. Then our next-door neighbor, Angie, came by. No one else came, so my mother led us in some Bible songs, and then we started our lesson. We asked a lot of questions, and the class was actually interesting and even fun. After two hours, we had pizza, cookies, and punch.

Word must have spread because the next day about ten kids showed up. Soon more attended, and toward the end of the week we had about twenty kids. Each day, we all sang, laughed, asked questions, and learned a lot about the Bible. Clint and I no longer felt embarrassed about vacation Bible school, and in fact, we were a little proud of what our mother was trying to do. During this time of closeness and sharing, all of us seemed to look at each other in a different light. We made new friends and became closer with old ones. It was great.

One day, almost twenty years later, my friend Terri told me how much that summer and Bible school had meant to her. I was surprised. I knew that the experience had meant a lot to me, but I never really understood how much it meant to the other kids. I felt proud of my mother for starting the Bible school. She really made a difference in a lot of kids' lives.

Sometimes it may feel awkward to reach out to others, especially if we don't think they will accept us. Reach out anyway—you never know who you might touch and what kind of positive change it may have in their life.

Running Away

All my life, I've had the pleasure and pain of having an older brother. My brother, Clint, and I are twenty-one months apart. So, throughout my childhood, I always had someone to play with, rain or shine. But that someone was also known to pick on me, tease me, and boss me around. Sometimes it felt as if we'd be stuck together like glue for the rest of our lives.

Clint would always come up with things for us to do, and these things were usually either dangerous or downright stupid. For instance, one time the light bulb in my Easy-Bake Oven (a toy oven that really baked) went out. Clint decided we could still use the oven if we could somehow relight the bulb. He remembered seeing my mother use a match to ignite the pilot light on our gas stove, so he tried this technique with my toy oven. Everything blew up (including my father when he found out!).

I always did everything Clint told me to do. Some of you are probably wondering why. It's simple. He was older (but not necessarily wiser). My parents said that when they weren't around, Clint was in charge. I, therefore, had to listen to and obey him. But all of this changed one summer when I was nine.

At that time, my mother decided that my brother and I were getting too old for baby-sitters. She put us in a summer camp about a mile and a half away from our home. I remember we had to cross two busy highways while driving there.

Clint hated the camp and thought the food they served was terrible. I, on the other hand, enjoyed the camp but agreed on the criticism of the food. One day, Clint came up with a plan to run away from the camp. He said it would be easy and that Mom wouldn't care as long as we got home safely. I felt he was stretching the truth a little here and figured that if I ignored the plan, he would eventually forget about it. Wrong!

We were eating lunch at camp one day, and Clint came up to me and said, "Let's get out of here." I looked at him and asked, "Are you sure this is such a good idea?" He nodded and grabbed my hand. Somehow, we sneaked past the teacher on the playground, and before I knew it, we were heading home.

Clint had always been very observant and, true to his nature, he'd memorized the route for us to take home. It was a long walk, and even the thought of the camp's food sounded more appealing than the tiring trek home. After what seemed like hours, we reached our front door at last. We had made it across two highways and countless streets. But one thing my brother didn't happen to think about while hatching this escape plan was how we would get into our locked house without a key.

"I know!" he said. "I'll break the basement window, and you can crawl through."

"Why do I have to be the stunt girl?" I asked.

He replied, "Because you're smaller, and it will be easier for you."

You can imagine the look I gave him. But I did what he said. After he had broken the window, I crawled through. I got a few minor cuts in the process, but I was okay. Then our Doberman Pinscher mistook me for a burglar and tried to attack. In the nick of time, the dog realized who I was—I survived!

I went to the back door and let Clint in. We played for a while, and then we heard our mother's car pull up. "Run for it!" my brother yelled. I was confused. He had told me we wouldn't get into trouble, so what was he worrying about now?

But we did get in trouble: BIG trouble. That evening, we watched in horror as my dad brought out his spanking belt. After the running away incident, my parents decided to let me use my own judgment about whether to obey Clint. They also warned him about leading me down the wrong path.

From that day on, I no longer had to obey my brother's wishes. I started making my own decisions. This was my first step toward learning how to be in charge of myself.

4

Coping

A wise man once said:

"People may tell you that you can't do this or you'll never do that, but it's up to you to say, 'Yes I can!'"

Clinton A. Walker

Cut from the Team

Sometimes, when you're playing a sport during gym class, you begin to think that you're really good. At least, that's how I felt in my gym class when I was fifteen, especially when we played softball. The truth is, half of the kids didn't even try to play. And the others could only play about as well as I could. In other words, I didn't have much competition.

I really liked to bat and to play first base. When it was my turn to bat, I usually hit the ball and got to base. So, naturally I thought I was a pretty good softball player. In fact, I thought I was good enough to try out for the girls' softball team, and that's just what I did.

Before tryouts, I bought a glove and then I headed for the practice field. I thought I recognized a lot of the girls, but some were unfamiliar to me. I noticed right away that these players were good. They threw the ball much faster and harder than my gym classmates did. For a moment, I actually thought I might have accidentally gone to the boys' practice field, and then I realized that was silly. These were girls—girls with big muscles and strong hands and amazing throwing arms. I tried not to appear intimidated. "After all," I told myself, "I'm the player who always gets a base hit in gym class."

First, we went through a number of drills and exercises. Then Coach Curtain made us play a game against each other. When I was batting, the pitcher threw the ball so fast I hardly saw it coming. I struck out a couple of times, then finally managed to make it to first base . . . on a walk. (Well, it still counted.)

When the other team was up to bat, I quickly claimed my favorite position—first base. I couldn't wait to show the coach my skills. The first batter hit a grounder that came right to me—an easy out. I thought, "I may have had some trouble with my batting, but I sure know how to play first base." The next batter hit the ball to second base, and my teammate made the catch. She threw the ball (or, should I say, put it on a rocket and shot it) to me. That ball came so fast, I did the first thing that came to my mind—jumped out of the way. Everyone just looked at me like I was from outer space.

At the end of each practice, we all had to race about fifty yards to show how fast we ran. Finally, I could show people that I had a skill. I always finished first, and Coach Curtain was impressed.

When it was time to announce who had made the team, the coach began calling out names. I waited and waited, but my name wasn't called. I'd been cut from the team. I was devastated; I thought at the very least I'd be able to ride the bench. "What about all those years of practice in gym class?" I thought. "Don't they count for something?"

I felt angry and embarrassed that I had gotten cut from the softball team. I was even mad at Coach Curtain for not just letting me be on the team, despite my lack of hitting and catching skills. The coach pulled me aside and told me that he was sorry he couldn't put me on the team. "You aren't a softball player, Cassandra," he said. "But you *are* a fast runner. I know that track season has already started, but I told the track coach about your running, and she's willing to take a look at you. Maybe you can be on the track team."

My first reaction was, "Forget it, I'll never try out for anything again." I just figured there was no point, and that I might fail again. Besides, I had never thought about being on the track team before and wasn't sure I even wanted to be a runner. But, as I thought about it some more, I realized that I enjoyed running and was pretty fast. I swallowed my pride and tried to forgive Coach Curtain. Then I went out for track and made the team. During track season, I realized I was good, and I won a lot of races and medals.

Coach Curtain was wise enough to know that, in order for me to succeed, I had to play a sport in which I had some talent and potential. Softball just wasn't my thing. Although at first I was hurt and angry about not making the softball team, I began to accept the coach's decision. Later, I was even thankful that Coach Curtain had seen my potential and suggested that I go out for track. I learned that I can't be good at everything and that I needed to focus on my strengths. I'm just glad I had someone there to show me the way.

Do you have a special skill or interest? If you do, go out there and show people what you can do! Try out for a sport, join an art class, write an article or story, learn to play an instrument, or get involved in an acting class. If you never try and experiment, you'll never know what your real talents are or how far you can go with them in life.

Maybe you've tried out for something but didn't make it (like me, with softball). Don't think of yourself as a failure. Keep trying or find your other, hidden talents. Throughout your life, you'll find that your willingness to take chances and put yourself on the line can lead you to successes you never imagined were possible.

Stories from My Life

Never Give Up

Whenever someone is stricken with a serious medical problem, it's hard for loved ones and other people to cope and to understand what the person is going through. A young girl who wrote to me told me about her personal experience with a potentially life-threatening brain tumor, and her story really touched and inspired me. It is her hope that other young people will learn from her experiences. Here is her story, in her own words.

My name is Sayeh Nikpay. I am fourteen years old. Before April 1995, I was your normal twelve-year-old girl. Then I was diagnosed with a brain tumor. It has changed my life.

Two or three years ago, I started getting headaches once or twice a week. I remember I would just take Advil or wait them out. But then the headaches started getting more frequent and more intense. On average, I would get them once a day. Over-the-counter medications didn't help anymore. My father is a cluster-migraine patient (a migraine is a *very* severe and painful headache), so luckily my understanding parents believed me when I told them how serious my headaches were.

One morning in March, I got such a bad headache that I couldn't stay at school. My head was pounding, and everything bothered me—light, noise, even my friends trying to comfort me. My mother picked me up right away, and I rested in the dark at my grandma's house. The pain was so bad I felt like crying, screaming, or hitting my head against the wall. I threw up several times. After that, my parents decided to take me to a neurologist—a physician who specializes in diseases of the nervous system.

It was my sixth-grade year, and I went to a pediatric neurologist in Minneapolis, Minnesota. The doctor asked a lot of questions about my headaches, and he tested my coordination by watching me look up and down, walk back and forth, and walk on my heels and toes. He scheduled a CAT scan for me, which is not unusual on the first visit. Neurologists want to see what they're working with so they can rule out the possibility of a tumor. The doctor gave me a little book showing and explaining each of the scanning and X-ray machines. A CAT scanner looks like a big doughnut with a long table going through the doughnut. It's a way to take pictures of the inside of the human body.

The next day, my mom got a telephone call from the neurologist. He said they had found an abnormal blood vein in my head and that I would have to come in for an MRI (Magnetic Resonance Imaging) test.

That's when I started to get nervous (not because of the vein, but because of the MRI). The MRI is like a long, dark, narrow tunnel with a table in the center. You lay on the table inside. You are not supposed to move at all, even your eyes. To keep your head in place, they put a device that looks like a welder's mask over your face. There are loud clunking and clanking noises. It lasts for about an hour. Many people feel claustrophobic when getting an MRI.

I told some of my teachers and some of my friends about having to get an MRI. They were a bit surprised. Two of my friends knew how nervous I was, and on the day before my MRI, they gave me a card and a stuffed animal. The day of my MRI, my mom and I left for the clinic in the morning. I was nervous when we got there, but the nice nurses made me feel better. I had been told there weren't going to be any needles involved, so I relaxed a bit. I had to dress in one of those silly hospital gowns. I put all of my clothes in a locker and, with my new stuffed animal in hand, waited outside the MRI room with my mom. They called me in and explained what would happen. When they put me on the table, they gave me earplugs and a round ball attached to a cord, which I could squeeze if I had to get out!

They slid me in and started the machine. It was dark and noisy, but I wasn't worried at all. My mom squeezed my foot the whole way through to let me know she was there. I spent the longest hour of my life, counting the seconds that went by.

I was so happy when they pulled me out—I couldn't have been happier. Then, to my horror, they said the picture wasn't clear enough, so they had to do it over again. And to make matters worse, they had to give me an IV (intravenous, or needle and tube to inject you) filled with dye to get clearer test results. Because I was extremely afraid of needles, I was so disappointed I could have screamed! Luckily, I was still groggy from being in the machine, and the needle only hurt half as much as I expected. So, I went back into the MRI for another hour that seemed twice as long as the first one.

My mom and I went home to eat lunch after the test was over. I was playing the piano when we got a phone call. My mom answered. I kept playing the piano, not really listening. When I saw my mom hang up and start sobbing, I thought someone had died. I went to her and so did my father and brother. She told us that the doctors had found a tumor in my brain. Suddenly, everyone around me was crying except me. I just sort of stood there. I can't really remember what I was thinking . . . except that I told myself not to cry. And I didn't. I asked myself, "Is crying going to change anything?"

I told my parents that I still wanted to go to school that afternoon. I planned to tell only my teacher and my best friend about the tumor, so nobody else would know. When I walked into the classroom, nobody was there except my teacher. The class was at choir practice. I told my teacher everything, saying, "I never thought this would happen to me." She said that it couldn't be possible. Oh, how I wished that were true.

The next day, my mom, dad, brother, and grandma came with me to see the neurologist. He said the tumor was located in my brain stem, in a place that is impossible to reach for a biopsy (tissue sample) or through surgery. The place where the tumor was growing was slightly affecting the flow of my cerebral fluid, which could mean a possible blockage of my spinal fluid. The neurologist recommended a shunt, which is a tube that can drain spinal fluid from your brain into your abdomen.

Over the next month, I told some of my friends and other teachers about my tumor. Everyone was very supportive. My friends and family prayed for me. People sent me cards and flowers. My teacher gave me a fourleaf-clover pendant for good luck on my MRI tests. Before I found out about my tumor, I didn't know how much people cared about me. It feels good to know that people are thinking of you before they go to sleep, and remembering you in their prayers.

I didn't think about my tumor very much. In fact, sometimes I totally forgot about it. My mind was on better things. I was looking forward to my trip to Greece at the end of May. And I had homework and lines to memorize for a play I was performing in. But sometimes I really started to think about it, late at night or when I was alone.

I was leaving for Greece two weeks before school let out. I had one more MRI scheduled on my last day of school. I decided that I would tell my class about the tumor before I left for Greece, because a whole summer would go by before I saw my classmates again. It was going to be hard to tell them, but I wanted to do it.

My second MRI went fine, except I got an IV in my arm. They gave me a sedative, so I slept through the long part of the test. When I woke up, it was done. We waited for about an hour or more for the pictures to come through. Finally, my neurologist received the results. In a month's time, the tumor hadn't grown at all. That really didn't mean anything because it would take a long time to grow anyway. But it was nice to hear something good for a change.

When we got back to my school, I sat in front of my class on the floor. I told them, while playing with my shoes, about why I had been gone and what the doctors had said. When I was finished I felt better, happier. Actually, I was sort of uncomfortable because my teacher and some of my friends were crying, but I was so happy and relieved. I was smiling and laughing a little. I think overall it was a pretty good last day of sixth grade for me.

Two days after that, I left for Greece and had a wonderful time. I made some friends and relaxed. We went swimming a lot and ate great food. I had lots of great experiences. We didn't even talk about my tumor.

A month or two after I got back home, I went to the Mayo Clinic, one of the best medical clinics in the world. It is located in Rochester, Minnesota, about an hour from my house. The doctors at Mayo asked me even more questions about my headaches and did more coordination tests than the first neurologist I had seen. When we talked with the neurosurgeon and neurologist there, they gave us all the facts. They couldn't tell if the tumor was cancerous or benign (not cancerous) yet, but hopefully we would know within two years.

They also said that I couldn't go more than two hours away from a hospital with a neurosurgeon on staff twenty-four hours a day. If I were to get a prolonged headache with nausea and drowsiness, it might be a symptom of my spinal fluid being blocked by the tumor and building up in my brain. I would have to be rushed to the hospital and get some of my spinal fluid drained.

If this happened, I would probably go to Mayo and get what they called a third ventriculostomy (where they cut a hole in the third ventricle of the brain to help drain the spinal fluid). The doctors said that if I didn't get my spinal fluid drained, I would get hydrocephalus (where fluid collects within the brain and puts pressure on it). This could permanently affect my learning and could become dangerous very quickly.

In December of 1996, I had another MRI test and received bad news. Although my tumor was not growing, there was a mechanical obstruction in my brain, and I was diagnosed with hydrocephalus. In February 1997, I had to have brain surgery, which was risky and meant having part of my head shaved. I was out of school for about three weeks. Now I have a shunt (that I'll have for the rest of my life), and it runs from the top of my head, through my body, and into my abdomen.

My life has changed so much in so little time. I've had to get MRI tests, go to doctor appointments, and listen to what could happen to me, which has all taken a lot of courage. But still I have managed to be an optimist and never let any of it get me down.

About the best advice I could give to anyone about anything is this: You have to be an optimist. You can't be yourself or live your life if you feel that you have a black cloud hovering over your head.

If people treat you differently or tease you because you are different, it just means that they are insecure. In some ways, this can be an opportunity to become a stronger person. I hope to have the chance to be of help to other kids going through experiences like mine. A medical problem may change your life, but you are still the same nice person inside. Always remember that!

Today, Sayeh still has the tumor but is doing well. She says that her life has more meaning, now that she knows how important life truly is. "I want to encourage children all over the world to never give up, never," says Sayeh. I hope her message helps you to never give up on yourself.

Self-Defense

After baseball season ended, my parents decided it was important for my brother, Clint, and I to have an activity that we could do together for a few hours a week. In other words, we were getting on our parents' nerves and they needed some time away from us.

My mom soon found what she said was the perfect activity—karate. "What? They must be joking," I thought. I told myself that there was no way I was going to hop around on some mat in bare feet, kicking sweaty people and screaming, "Ha Ya!" It was bad enough having to watch karate movies with my brother, let alone actually be in a karate class with him. Besides, I was worried I might hurt myself, or worse, break a fingernail! "That settles it," I thought, "Forget karate. How about something more civilized, like ballet?"

About a week later, we were in the car on the way to karate class, and I was pouting. My mother told me that it was important for me to learn some form of self-defense. She said I only had to stay in the class until I earned my yellow belt, which would take about two months. My brother, on the other hand, was as excited as he could be. After all, he loved karate, and this class would give him a good excuse to kick me. As I stared out the windshield, I convinced myself that I wouldn't like the class at all.

We entered the class, and I noticed all sorts of trophies and awards that the instructors had earned. The room was musty and warm, and it smelled like sweaty feet. We had to take off our shoes, and we were given uniforms to change into.

There was only one other girl in the class. I was so glad to have a soul mate—someone who'd understand me, someone else who wouldn't like the idea of jumping around in white pajamas, getting kicked and chopped. In the dressing room, I introduced myself to her and said, "I don't really want to be here, how about you?" Her reply was surprising to me: "I've been trying to get my parents to let me join this class for two years. I can't wait to get out there and get going!" So much for soul mates.

In our first class, we went over the rules and tried some karate stances. Then we were told to line up against the wall. The instructor said that it was very important for a student of karate to have a good mind and a strong body, and that at the end of every class we would be punched in the stomach to help strengthen our muscles.

"Excuse me, did he say *punched* in the stomach?!" I said to my brother.

"Yes," he replied, grinning broadly.

At that moment, I knew I had to get out of there, but it was too late. The punching had already started.

All I could hear was, "Ooh, eek, ugh," then my own yell of, "OUCH!"

My parents didn't even flinch when I told them what had happened in class. "I'm sure they won't do anything to really hurt you," my father said.

"Yeah, sure they won't," I thought, "*He* doesn't have to get knocked around like a punching bag, so what does he care?"

Despite my whining, we kept going to karate class two days a week for two hours a day. After a while, I started getting the hang of it. I still didn't like the class, though, and I couldn't wait until I could quit.

One evening, my mom told us she had an appointment and that she would be a little late picking us up from our next karate class. She gave us some money to get something at the hot dog stand after class, and she instructed us to wait for her there.

After class, Clint and I were standing at the corner waiting to cross the street and go to the hot dog stand. I noticed three teenage boys with long, stringy hair heading our way. Something told me they were up to no good. I told my brother, and he started to stuff his money in his pocket. I realized it was too late for that because the teenage boys would see what I was doing. So, I just kept my money clenched in my fist.

The boys caught up with us before the light changed. "Give us your money or else," they said to my brother. Clint had a strange look on his face. He reluctantly handed over his money. Then the boys ran away, laughing.

Coping

My brother and I ran across the street. Clint had tears in his eyes, and I knew it was because he felt helpless. After all, those boys were a lot bigger than we were, and they outnumbered us. When our mother came to pick us up and heard what had happened, she was furious. She drove around for about an hour looking for the teenage boys, but we never found them.

Later that night, when we were getting ready for bed, my brother told me: "Even though we now know karate, there was nothing I could do about those boys. I thought that if I knew karate, I could beat anyone. Now I feel like I can't even protect myself."

I could tell he felt bad; he was used to always being the strong and protective one. Then I remembered something we had learned in karate. I said to Clint: "Remember our instructor said that part of karate is knowing when *not* to fight. You knew you were outnumbered, and if you had resisted giving the money to those boys, you could have gotten hurt and I could have, too. You were the winner today. Those boys may have been older, but you were the one who was more mature." I couldn't believe I said that to him. And I really couldn't believe that I had learned a valuable lesson in the karate class I was so determined to hate.

What I realized that day was: Every experience, no matter how new or strange or scary, can really teach you something. I had been learning things in karate class, despite my complaints. After the incident with the teenage boys, both my brother and I recognized that sometimes the best form of self-defense is to walk away from a dangerous situation.

When something scary happens to you, your natural reaction might be to withdraw, pretend it didn't happen, or feel guilty that you couldn't control the situation. But it's better to talk about it with someone you love and trust. I'm glad that Clint and I told my mother about those teenage boys, instead of acting like nothing had happened. And I'm proud that my brother admitted to me that he was feeling helpless. I hope my words made him feel better.

Good-bye Forever
(In memory of Mrs. Carson)

In kindergarten, I was just as talkative as I am now, and that's probably why the kids called me "Cassandra Talker" instead of Cassandra Walker. I thought it was my duty to let the other kids know how friendly I was, so I was very surprised when the teacher sent home a note to my parents asking them to make me . . . well, shut up.

I remember the teacher seating me next to a boy named Keith. He was very shy, and the teacher must have known I would get no conversation out of him. Up until that point, my only other interaction with Keith had been on the first day of school. When he came into the classroom with his mother, he had a lunch box and I told him, "You don't need a lunch box in kindergarten—we go home at noon." He looked at me, then turned to his mother and started crying. "Oops!" I thought.

I also knew that Keith was very close to his mother. Every day for the first week or so of kindergarten, he would hold on to her and cry, asking her not to leave him. All of the other kids would stand around and look at Keith, kind of shocked by his display of emotion. Of course, I thought it was my job to try and talk to him and cheer him up. Well, it didn't work. In fact, I think it made him more upset, so I gave up.

Sitting next to him each day, I often tried to get a conversation going. He didn't say a word, though, and just kept coloring with his jumbo crayons, never looking at me. Then one day, we were going to make Christmas cards for our parents and I heard a voice say, "I'm going to make mine real pretty for my mom." I looked around to see who had spoken and, sure enough, it was Keith. From that time on, if I mentioned his mom I could get him to talk. I learned that he was very smart, and we soon became friends. Over the next four years, we remained classmates and grew closer. His mom sometimes worked in the lunchroom at our school and was very well liked.

At the beginning of fifth grade, my parents transferred me to a school near my home. I thought for sure I would never see any of my old classmates again. But on the second day of school, in walked Keith. His parents had transferred him also. We stayed close, but by the middle of the following year, my family had moved and I had to say good-bye to all of my friends, teachers, and classmates.

Over the next few years, I lost touch with Keith and his family. Then one day, I ran into a former classmate of mine. We started talking about old times, and I asked him if he had seen Keith lately. He said he had and that

Keith was doing much better now. I asked, "What do you mean *now?*" "Didn't you hear?" he answered, "Keith's mom died of cancer a year or two ago." I was stunned. This meant that Keith's mom had died when he was only twelve years old.

I started to cry for my friend and his family. I couldn't imagine how awful it must have been to say good-bye to a loved one. I'd had a hard enough time just switching schools and leaving old friends behind. But death meant good-bye forever. Keith must have been devastated. His mom wouldn't be there to help him with his homework, teach him to drive, go to his graduation, or see him get married.

I thought about Keith for the next thirteen years, and I often prayed that he was okay. When I was in my twenties, I finally saw Keith again, and I asked him how he was doing. He said things were hard for a while after his mother had died, but he was now doing very well. Keith said that what had helped him to keep going was the thought that his mom loved him and would have wanted him to continue being a good student. She would have wanted him to do his best in life. By this time, Keith had gone on to medical school and was excited about his future. I thought that his mother would be very proud.

Some of you have lost a parent or another loved one. It's tough, I know, but don't let it pull you down too far. You still have a wonderful life to lead, and that loved one would want you to live your life to the fullest. If you're having a hard time coping, contact your school counselor or another adult who can help you to find a support group for young people who are going through the same things you are. Don't give up.

5

Growing Pains

"If you live by what other people think, it may mean you aren't thinking for yourself."

Odessa Floyd Walker

Behind the Wheel

There are all types of milestones when growing up, such as when you learn to walk, when you lose your first tooth, when you first start school, when you fall in love for the first time, when you begin high school, and one of the most exciting ones: when you get your driver's license.

I wasn't particularly interested in driving until I hit age fifteen. Some kids on my block had been talking about wanting to drive since we were about twelve. But I was content with my good old ten-speed bike. It took me everywhere I needed to go, and I didn't have to spend much money to keep it running. But when I became a sophomore in high school, I started to realize that I was almost a legal adult using the same mode of transportation as a seven-year-old. It was time for a change.

In most schools, driver's education starts with a classroom orientation and testing. "This part is a breeze," I thought. The questions were straightforward and to the point. I remember thinking that if actual driving was as easy as the classroom part, I was going to burn some rubber.

After six weeks of driver's education, we signed up for summertime "Behind the Wheel" training. This was in March, so we had several months to practice with our parents or other licensed drivers before we started Behind the Wheel with our teacher. Well, my parents weren't too happy about the idea of me driving, especially when they were in the same car. The words *dangerous* and *life-threatening* kept coming up. So, my brother was assigned the job of teaching me how to drive. He wasn't the world's most patient person, and he had no problem letting me know that he didn't appreciate this job my parents had given him. I felt nervous around Clint, and it was hard for me to relax and get comfortable with driving.

Before I knew it, Behind the Wheel class was starting. I knew I still needed more training, and I was worried. But two other students, Lucille and Rose, who were my cheerleading teammates and friends, got assigned to the same student-driver car as I did. I began to feel better about the whole situation because my friends were right there with me. The one thing I didn't know was that they both had been practicing a lot and were pretty good drivers.

On our starting day, Lucille was chosen to try driving the course first. She whizzed around the corners and in and out of the traffic cones like a seasoned veteran. Next came Rose, and she had no problems with parking, switching lanes, or making turns. Our teacher, Mr. Johnston, said, "Hey, you girls are pretty good. This should be the easiest class I've ever had to teach."

Then it was my turn to drive. Because I hadn't had that much practice, being on the road intimidated me. Right away, I got the feeling that Mr. Johnston thought I drove like his grandmother . . . before she got her glasses. To make a long story short, after my turn Mr. Johnston looked at me and commented, "I take back what I said earlier."

During every Behind the Wheel training session, it seemed as though Rose and Lucille were rapidly improving. But I was learning much more slowly. In fact, I was just happy when I remembered to stop turning the steering wheel after making a right-hand turn. Out of sheer frustration and concern that I was giving my teacher an ulcer, I begged my parents to let me practice driving more often at home. They agreed, and my mother started taking me out after she got home from work. By this time, only two weeks remained until the day I dreaded: The Day of the Final Driving Exam. I told myself that on that day, I had to get everything right.

On the big day, I was very nervous. I remember praying all the way to the school parking lot. Lucille and Rose were already there, looking as cool as cucumbers. We all piled into the car, and Lucille, the best driver of the three of us, went first. She started off great, but about halfway through the test, she started making mistakes that she normally didn't make. She knocked down cones and couldn't correctly parallel park. Mr. Johnston was surprised, but he told her she was probably just nervous.

She finally finished the test, and then it was Rose's turn. She had trouble with the test, too. I was shocked and scared. I thought, "If *they're* nervous and messing up, how am *I* possibly going to pass this test?"

My turn came next. I took the wheel, and my palms immediately began to sweat. I looked at the long row of cones in front of the car and cautiously approached each one, weaving between them like an expert. I was surprised and felt elated. Next, I had to change lanes and come to a stop. No problem!

But the real challenge was parallel parking. I took a deep breath, glanced in the rearview mirror and side mirrors, and made my move. I backed up and began to pull into the space between the cones. I stopped a few times during the process to adjust my hands on the wheel, but within a matter of minutes, I had successfully completed the toughest assignment of the day. For the first time since I'd started learning to drive, I parallel parked *perfectly*. I got a perfect score on the test, and I was on cloud nine!

Everyone, including me, was surprised. I had been the one making mistakes all summer, and now, when it really counted, I did everything right. Even Mr. Johnston congratulated me. When I got home, I ran straight to my doubting brother's room and showed him my score. He smiled and said, "There must be some mistake. . . . Just kidding! Good job."

Becoming a good driver takes a lot of time and practice. You might have trouble on the written exam or on

Stories from My Life

driving the course, but eventually you'll get it right. Whether you ace your driving exam on the first try or have to make several attempts, stay confident in yourself.

Always have the courage to keep trying. You may not always be successful at the things you try, but if you do your best and believe in yourself, you'll always have *that* to be proud of. Don't give up! And that goes for anything in life.

How Embarrassing!

One of my most embarrassing moments occurred during second grade. Here's what happened: My brother had aspirations of becoming a world-class barber and decided he needed a client to practice on. And who do you think he picked? You guessed it—me. Clint told me he was going to use pretend scissors. He lied.

Unfortunately for me, Clint cut off my center ponytail (the one with the most hair) on the back of my head. By the time he had finished this "haircut," it was bedtime, so I didn't get a chance to look in the mirror to see what he'd done. I just climbed into bed and went to sleep. The way he'd said "Oops!" and took off should have alerted me that something was very wrong.

The next morning, my mother came to wake me up, only to find my nicely braided ponytail, with a pink ribbon still on it, lying on my bedroom floor. I woke up to my mom's shouts of, "Oh, my goodness . . . Clint, what have you done!?" Needless to say, my mom wasn't impressed with my brother's newfound occupation.

I was, of course, very upset. But I think Mom was even more upset because she was the one who had to find a creative way to cover up my new bald spot.

Fortunately, afros were in style, so she cut one of her afro wigs and made an afro puff to stick on my bald spot. She placed it strategically at the center of the back of my head, attaching it ever so delicately to my leftover hair, using bobby pins.

"There," she said. "Now, if the wind doesn't blow too hard, you'll be just fine." I remember walking to school at a very slow pace so as not to create a gush of air.

For a while, no one knew about my condition but me. Then one day, during a very active recess, I went one way and my afro puff went the other. My secret was exposed! The other kids immediately began to laugh and call me "Cassandra Bald Spot." I started to cry.

For the rest of the school year, or until my hair grew back (whichever came first), I was called "Baldy" and every other name having to do with hair loss. I was even told I looked more like my father, who had been losing his hair for fifteen years. What a compliment.

I thought I would die of embarrassment, but I didn't. I actually lived to tell the story, and now I can even laugh about the incident.

Believe it or not, everyone has had an embarrassing moment at one time or another. You're not the only one. The next time you find yourself in one of those oh-so-embarrassing situations, try not to let it get you down. Your natural reaction might be to cry uncontrollably or run away, never to return. But try to just laugh it off instead. By laughing at yourself, you'll show people that you have a sense of humor and good self-esteem.

Stories from My Life

Stick Up for Yourself

Peer pressure was a part of my life all the way through my college years. Then I finally wised up and started living life for me and not for everyone else.

During my sophomore year in college, my parents bought me my first car. I recall that someone once told me, "You are what you drive." In that case, I was a 1980 Buick Skylark Hatchback—and a used one at that. I was so proud of my car that I couldn't wait to show it to my friends.

I called my friends and told them my news. Then I drove my Skylark to some of my friends' homes to show it off. But many of my friends weren't nearly as impressed and excited as I was. Some of them even had the nerve to say, "Oh, I thought you had a *new* car." (These remarks came from people who had no mode of transportation of their own, I might add.)

Some of my other friends were very happy for me and congratulated me on my new "wheels." Yet, the negative comments began to chip away at my self-esteem. I thought more and more about the fact that my car was older and used. I wondered why I didn't have a brand-new car to ride around in. Soon I stopped liking my car, and I even stopped driving it as much.

It didn't make a difference to me anymore that my car didn't actually look old. In fact, it looked almost brand-new. It just wasn't as sleek as the newest models on the road. I pouted for days.

I didn't realize how truly blessed I was to even have a car to drive. I should have been proud that my parents bought this car for me, that they paid cash, and that they were still able to pay for my college education. I didn't consider the fact that my friends who had new cars were working full-time to make their car payments. And here I was, pouting like a child.

I finally understood that I was living according to other people's standards, not my own. And I was basing my feelings on what other people thought or said. So, I started my car again. From that point on, if anyone ever said something negative about my car, I simply said, "Well, it's mine and I like it. That's all that matters." And I was right.

It's hard to stand up to criticism sometimes. But you can do it! Concentrate on being yourself, taking pride in what you have and what you do, and believing that you know what's right for you.

Born to Swim

Some people were born to swim, and I believe I'm one of them. I've enjoyed swimming ever since I started taking lessons at the age of three. I thought of it as recreation and never envisioned myself swimming in the Olympics or anything. My dad, however, thought I was a female Mark Spitz (the seven-time Olympic gold medalist for swimming in 1972).

My parents enrolled my brother and me in a summer swimming program at a local high school when I was about nine years old. It was great for me, but my brother was scared to death and had to be threatened by the instructor to jump off the diving board for a skills test. Finally, I had a chance to tease *him* about something!

My love for swimming kept growing as I did, and every summer when I would go away for a week to summer camp, I took various swimming skills tests until I finally became a junior lifeguard. I even learned how to perform CPR (cardiopulmonary resuscitation) on drowning victims. There was no other athletic activity I enjoyed more than swimming, except maybe cheerleading.

The better I got at swimming, the more my father saw star potential. So, it didn't surprise me when he suggested that I go out for the freshman swim team when I entered high school. I thought it was a great idea since swimming came so naturally to me. As it turns out, I made the team!

The first day of practice was pretty easy. We just went over some rules and got to know other members of the team. On the second day of practice, I was late, so the team had already finished the first part of their workout. While they were on the second part, the coach told me I had to catch up. He said, "Give me fifty, then go over with the rest of the team."

I figured that was easy enough—fifty yards in swimming was just the length of the pool and back. After I'd finished, I joined the rest of the team. I had been with them for about twenty minutes when the coach noticed me.

"Did you already finish the fifty?" he asked.

"Of course," I said.

He replied, "Wow, you are really fast, Walker. I'm glad to see that."

My dad was elated when I told him what the coach had said. My father was also pleased to hear that I was enjoying swimming with an organized team. This was the first time I had ever swam with a real team; all of my other swimming experiences had been at camp or at lessons.

The next day at practice, the coach wanted to time me, so he asked me to do fifty again. I swam the length of the pool and back as fast as I could, and then I stopped.

He looked at me and said, "Keep going."

Stories from My Life

I was puzzled and answered, "That was fifty yards, Coach."

"I didn't want fifty yards!" he yelled. "I wanted fifty *laps!* No wonder you finished so fast yesterday. You owe me forty-eight more laps, so finish up."

I was shocked. I had never attempted fifty laps in a row. What did he think I was—a *dolphin?* I somehow finished the fifty, and I was actually sweating in the pool. I was so tired that my head was spinning, and practice wasn't even over yet.

After a few weeks of this, I didn't like swimming anymore. I hoped that once our swim meets started, I would enjoy the competition. But I found out that I didn't like competing either. Ironically, I kept becoming a better swimmer, and I was even put on the varsity level for several meets. This made my father as proud as a peacock. He showed up at every competition, cheering me on with dreams of an Olympic gold medal. I had to pretend that I was just as happy as he was. Finally, the season ended and I felt relieved.

In the spring of my freshman year, I joined the track team and found out I was pretty good. My track coach suggested that I try out for the cross country team in the fall to get in shape for the upcoming track season. Cheerleading tryouts were also held in the fall, and I really enjoyed cheerleading. But fall was swimming season, too. I was worried because I knew my dad wouldn't allow me to quit the swim team in favor of another activity.

At the beginning of sophomore year, my dad and my track coach began pressuring me. My dad wanted me to go out for the swim team, and the track coach kept asking me when I was going to sign up for cross country. I stalled, and the deadline for both tryouts passed. My dad and my track coach were very angry with me. But I knew deep inside that I didn't want to swim or run—I wanted to be a cheerleader. Although I felt guilty about this choice, I knew it would make me happy. I had to please myself, not other people.

The day of cheerleading tryouts arrived, and I did a great job. I stayed with cheerleading for the rest of my high school years. I never joined the swim team again, but I did run track every spring. After a while, my dad forgave me and realized I had to do what made me happy. I never had any regrets.

Sometimes your parents or other adults will have big dreams for your future. They may imagine that you'll be a sports star, a famous celebrity, or even president. As a result, you may feel pushed and pulled in directions you don't want to go. Trust yourself. In sports, as in life, you have to do what makes *you* feel good and special. It's your future, and you have to make decisions that are right for you, no matter what other people may think or wish.

Take a Stand

You know, it's one thing to put *yourself* in jeopardy because of peer pressure (for instance, shoplifting because your friends do, or smoking just to go along with the crowd). But have you ever done something your peers pressured you into, and it ended up hurting *someone else?*

A boy named Alvin, who went to my high school, had just this kind of experience. He and some of his friends didn't have anything to do one night, so they decided to go for a ride in Alvin's car around downtown Chicago. After a tour of the city, the group headed home, winding through some of the nicer neighborhoods around town. While cruising, they came upon a beautiful home with a very expensive car parked in the driveway. One of Alvin's friends asked him to pull over.

"What for, man?" Alvin asked.

"I just want to get a better look at that car," his friend replied.

Alvin felt nervous about pulling over, but he didn't want to say no to his best friend. So he stopped the car.

Alvin's friend then said, "Hey, man, let's cut that car's tires. It would be funny if the owner came out tomorrow and had flat tires. After all, he can afford new tires if he's driving that car."

"No," said Alvin. "I don't want to do that. Why don't you just get back in the car?"

His friend didn't budge. "Chill out. Don't be such a baby."

Alvin knew vandalism was wrong, but the other guys in the car were going along with the plan. Alvin didn't want to go against their wishes or to speak out again. He watched as one tire after the next was slashed.

Suddenly, a man appeared on the front steps of the home and started screaming at Alvin and his friends. Alvin's buddy, who had been slashing the tires, jumped back in the car and yelled, "Let's get out of here!" They sped off quickly, with the man chasing behind them on foot.

"Whew, Alvin, we almost got caught, but the main thing is we didn't," said his friends.

The next day, Alvin's dad asked him to sit down and have a talk. His dad was very upset because he had just gotten off the phone with the police. The man in Chicago had written down Alvin's license plate number and reported him as a vandal. Alvin couldn't say a word in his own defense. "I was sure we'd gotten away," thought Alvin. "The guy didn't even see my face."

Alvin's parents now had to pay the bill for the man's new tires. The boy who'd slashed the tires was also caught. His mother had to pay for part of the new tires, too. Alvin lost his driving privileges for a long time and had to earn the money to pay his parents back. He learned that no matter how slick you think you are, it's easy to get caught when you're doing something illegal.

More importantly, Alvin learned that it wasn't right to hurt other people or their property. When Alvin told me this story, he said: "The thing that bothered my dad the most about the whole incident was that I was so insensitive to the man in Chicago. I was involved in vandalizing his property, and I didn't even seem to care how it would affect him. What if he had a medical emergency that very next day and needed to get to the hospital quickly, but found his tires were flat?" Alvin then told me he had learned that one of the worst kinds of peer pressure is the kind that causes you to hurt not only yourself but innocent people as well.

It's not easy to stand up for what's right when you're with your friends, or when you're being pressured by your peers. But my father always told me, "If you don't stand for something, you will fall for anything." Learn to take a stand.

6

Understanding Others

*"Look for the good so that
you may enjoy it."*

Ethiopian proverb

Don't Judge a Person by His Title

When I was only about ten, I learned something that has stuck with me my whole life. I came to realize that it's not your job, or looks, or clothes, or belongings that make you special and important. What really counts is what you have inside you and the impact you have on other people's lives.

I went to a small, private Lutheran school until I was in fourth grade. The school had less then 200 students total, in grades kindergarten through eight. Because the school was so small, we were a close-knit group. The adults at the school included six full-time classroom teachers, a secretary, the principal, a librarian, the gym teacher, and the custodian, Mr. Clark.

Mr. Clark was a friendly man. He was always there when we got to school and was the last one to leave after the students and faculty had gone home. You could usually find him sweeping the hall or shoveling snow off the parking lot that served as our playground during recess. Mr. Clark was the person who fixed things, who kept the school clean, and who restocked the light bulbs, chalk, or any other items needed in the classrooms. He helped keep the school in tip-top shape.

While most of the teachers and other staff members wore suits or dresses to school, Mr. Clark always had on a pair of faded blue overalls—even on special days. A worn-out baseball cap sat propped up on his head. In the winter, he'd have on a scruffy brown overcoat, a black knit scarf, and a black hat with fake fur on the inside to keep his head warm. He wore oversized black rubber boots outdoors as he cleared away the snow, whistling his favorite hymn.

One day, I heard a group of older kids saying mean things about Mr. Clark. They were saying that he was dirty and poor. They said he wasn't smart, which was why he was a janitor, not a teacher. They also said he wore those faded overalls because he couldn't afford to buy anything else. Their words hurt me very deeply. "How could they say that about Mr. Clark?" I thought. In our school, we were taught to appreciate everyone— no matter what their race, religion, or background. I liked that message and couldn't understand why other kids in the school weren't respecting it.

Before long, more kids at school were making fun of Mr. Clark. They whispered about him in the hallways and laughed at him behind his back. Mr. Clark just kept on smiling and singing and greeting everyone each morning. He never showed whether he knew about the rumors.

At the end of the school year, we always had a big celebration in the parking lot. A huge pile of toys, wrapped in newspaper, was gathered in the lot. Each student was allowed to choose two of these gifts. We also received a bag of candy each, and we bobbed for apples in a huge pail of water that Mr. Clark had set up for us. After the celebration, we'd see Mr. Clark picking up the paper and trash that we'd left behind.

This particular year, as we eagerly awaited our annual celebration, the principal made a special announcement. He said he planned to give Mr. Clark a plaque to show the school's appreciation. Some of the kids started to snicker. The principal then told everyone that Mr. Clark had been the sole provider of all the toys, candy, and apples we received at the end of each school year.

The students couldn't believe it. Year after year, Mr. Clark had bought all of those gifts and never said a word about it. He never even expected a thank you. I was so amazed by his generosity and so angry at all those kids who had been saying that Mr. Clark was poor and dirty. And I was also mad at myself for not sticking up for Mr. Clark and reminding those kids about respect. We all realized that instead of buying fancy clothes and shoes for himself, Mr. Clark had spent his money on gifts for others. He had really made a difference in our lives. Thank you, Mr. Clark.

Teasing Isn't Funny

y the time I reached eighth grade, I'd heard every joke about being tall and skinny. I was called such names as "Too Tall Bones," "Olive Oyl," "Jolly Green Giant," etc. You get the picture. I just couldn't take it anymore. So, I felt relieved when another tall and skinny girl arrived at our school. She was a new seventh grader named Charlotte.

Charlotte was a quiet girl, with big eyes and long black hair. She walked down the halls with her books held close to her body. I'm sure she felt intimidated by the older kids, especially those who teased and mocked her as she walked by. Some of the eighth graders made what they referred to as "Charlotte jokes." They tried to come up with the funniest thing to say about how Charlotte walked or looked, or any other cruel remark. I wish I could say that I didn't laugh at these jokes, but I did. Although I didn't think the jokes were funny, I laughed just so those kids wouldn't tease me.

We noticed that Charlotte often didn't show up for school. And when we'd go outside for gym, Charlotte would watch us from a classroom window. For some reason, she didn't ever come outdoors during gym, and this just gave everyone another thing to tease her about.

One day, when we were outside, I hurt myself and had to go to the nurse's office. The nurse immediately gave me ice. (She always gave students ice. Whether you had cramps, a bump on your head, or internal bleeding, she first gave you ice.) I sat down with my ice-pack, and out of the corner of my eye, noticed that Charlotte was sitting near me. She smiled.

I looked around to make sure that no other kids could tease me for talking to Charlotte, and, seeing that the coast was clear, I smiled back. I decided to ask her how she was doing. She said she was fine and asked me if I had enjoyed gym class. I said I had, and then I found the courage to ask her why she never came outside during gym. What she said really had an effect on me and the way I treated people from that point on.

"I can't go outside because I can't do all of the physical activities required in gym," said Charlotte. "I have a bad heart, and I have to take medicine to keep it working. I've had to be in the hospital and doctors' offices all my life. That's why I miss so much school. But I don't fall behind in my school work because I study while I'm in the hospital or at home.

"It's hard for me to make friends because I'm absent from school so much. I know kids tease me, but that's because they don't understand me. I'm really a very nice person."

I found out in a short amount of time that Charlotte and I had a lot in common: We were both tall and got teased, we both had big feet, and we both were given ice whenever we went to see the nurse. I realized that Charlotte was nice and had a good sense of humor. After a few more minutes of talking, Charlotte had to go back to class. But before she left, she said: "On Friday, I'll be going to the hospital for open-heart surgery. I'm glad that I'll have this operation, even though it's kind of scary. After the operation, I'll be different. No more doctors all the time, no more needles, and no more pain. I'll be a new person. Will you pray for me and tell the other kids to also? It would make me feel good. I'll see you when I get back."

When I returned to class, I told my friends what had happened. Some of them were kind and said they would remember Charlotte in their prayers. But some of them weren't so kind and started telling new Charlotte jokes about how she had an "old lady heart."

On Friday, when Charlotte was going in for her operation, the principal told everyone to make get-well cards for Charlotte during homeroom. He said that on Monday he would give us the hospital name and the address so we could mail the cards. When Monday arrived, I could hardly wait to get the address so I could send the special card to my new friend. The principal's voice came over the loudspeaker, giving us an update on Charlotte.

Charlotte had been right when she said that after the operation there would be no more doctors, needles, or pain. We found out at that moment that Charlotte had died on the operating table. She was only eleven years old when she died. The classroom was quiet. We were all asked to walk to the gym, where we would have a mock funeral for Charlotte. Everyone was upset, and some kids were crying. I cried, too.

For weeks afterward, I'd find myself looking back at the classroom window during gym, as if Charlotte might be there watching us. I just couldn't believe she was gone.

I learned in a very hard way that other people's feelings count. I was so concerned about what others might think of *me* that I had completely ignored Charlotte's feelings and laughed at the jokes. If you see someone being made fun of, I hope you'll have more courage than I did and that you'll stick up for the person getting teased. Or, at the very least, don't join in the teasing or laughter. I regret that I never really got to know a wonderful person who probably could have taught me a lot about life.

Accepting Differences

My cousins Kim, Kaye, and Kelly lived next door to a boy who was mentally challenged. Although he was twelve, he was mentally at the level of a three-year-old. His name was Carl.

When I was about nine, I visited my cousins and was playing on their swingset. All of a sudden, I felt someone push me really high, and I became frightened. I turned around to look, and there was Carl, pushing me with all his might. He was quite strong, too.

I yelled, "Stop!" but he answered, "No," and continued. I began to cry.

My cousins came to my rescue. They talked to Carl calmly and made him stop pushing me. I got off the swing to face Carl.

At first, I didn't realize he was mentally challenged. But then he began speaking in a loud voice and yelling at my cousins. They didn't seem afraid of him, but his abrupt manner and strange voice sent chills up my spine. I had never met anyone like him, so I didn't understand how to react.

Every time I visited my cousins, Carl came by. Sometimes he threw rocks or sticks at us. Other times, he chased us and tried to hit us. I was very afraid of his rough behavior, and I was amazed that my cousins still treated him so nicely. They never teased him.

One day, my cousin Kaye told me that Carl had hit their mom (my Aunt Ethel) in the head with a brick. I was shocked. I figured that Carl must have gotten yelled at or spanked for what he'd done. But I found out that Aunt Ethel had simply talked to Carl and tried to explain to him why it wasn't right to hit or hurt others.

I had a lot of mixed emotions about Carl. Sometimes I feared him, and other times he made me angry. I tried to figure out why my cousins and aunt treated him so nicely, even after he had made trouble. What I came to understand was that they treated Carl with respect, and sometimes with caution. They knew he had limitations, and they tried to help him as much as they could. They didn't blame him for his behavior; instead, they tried to be caring. My Aunt Ethel and Uncle Floyd had taught my cousins the importance of loving people for who they are and not for who you want or expect them to be. This was a lesson I was now learning, too.

Flat Feet

When I was growing up, the girl who lived next door to us, Angie, had flat feet. This meant she had no arches in her feet, so she had to wear corrective shoes. These shoes were big, with a rounded toe and thick black heels. They were also a bright red color.

At that time, a popular TV show featured a clown named Bozo. Bozo wore big, round-toed, black-soled, RED shoes. You can guess what happened: Angie was nicknamed "Bozo the Clown" because of her corrective shoes.

I hated it when people teased Angie. I felt powerless to do anything about it, too. Angie was such a nice person, and she never bothered or harmed anyone. I couldn't understand why other kids thought it was okay to make fun of her.

Her flat feet made it difficult for her to run, jump rope, or do flips. When she tried to do these things, people laughed. Her feet always seemed to get in the way of having fun. To make matters worse, she was very tall for her age, which sometimes caused problems with her coordination. Both of us felt frustrated, and I kept wishing I could do something to help her.

Sometimes we'd practice doing cartwheels in her front yard, over and over again. I tried to show her the technique, but unfortunately, she didn't learn much. It was awkward teaching a girl nearly a foot taller than I was to turn her body upside down, stand on her hands, and swing her legs rapidly through the air.

But we kept trying because Angie wanted to join the cheerleading team. She had to be able to turn cartwheels and flips with ease. When cheerleading tryouts finally arrived, we felt ready, and we hoped that all of our hard work would pay off. When Angie stepped up before the judges, some of the other girls snickered, pointed at her shoes, and made fun of her coordination (or lack thereof).

I was so proud of the way Angie appeared confident, despite the jeers. When she performed her flip, she looked like a swan—until her legs got twisted up and she fell to the ground. But even then, she stood up, dusted herself off, and smiled at the judges. And she made the team.

Angie had to keep wearing her corrective shoes and to put up with the teasing. Still, she remained courteous and kind to everyone, even to people who called her "Bozo" and "Clown Feet." She continued to smile, to be playful, and to brighten people's days when she could. Her positive outlook on life really meant a lot to me.

People come in many different shapes, sizes, and colors. That's what makes us all unique and special. We need to try to respect our differences, rather than judge people for them. It's what's on the inside—not the outside—that really counts.

It's Better to Give Than to Receive

Every Christmas and birthday, my brother and I would make our wish lists and give them to our parents. We took pride in going through the catalogs and finding just what we wanted (to save our parents time, of course), and we expected to receive at least 99 percent of what we asked for.

Now, I don't want you to get the impression that Clint and I were spoiled and selfish. In fact, our mother had always taught us that it was better to give than to receive. My brother and I thought we knew all about the spirit of giving. When it was time to give to people in need, Clint and I would search the very back of our shelves or dig down to the bottom of our dresser drawers to find something to offer—even if the items were broken or a little dirty. Yeah, we thought we were real generous.

One day, we told our mother about a boy and girl at school who didn't seem to have any winter clothing or warm jackets. Our mother was concerned about the family and came up with a plan. She told us that we were going to give them some of our clothing and coats, and that she would somehow offer these items anonymously. We thought this was a great idea.

She went to our closets and, to our amazement, started taking out our new or barely worn clothes and putting them into a box. "Wait!" we shouted. "Those are our good things!" Our mother replied, "Yes, I know that." She then said that she intended to give the family in need some of our nicer clothes because they had more use for them than we did.

Clint and I protested; we tried in vain to plead our case. We told our mother how much we needed our clothes, and beyond that, how much we *liked* our clothes. She just kept on packing the box. After a while, I was able to pull myself together and help her pack. But then she tossed in my prized *Happy Days* T-shirt (from my favorite television program), featuring none other than "Fonzie," the coolest guy on the show. I thought I'd never forgive her.

The next day, we took the box to the family's house. Our mom had attached a short note, but we didn't sign our names. We left the package on their doorstep, then went back home. Our mother said we should never tell any of the other kids at school about what we'd done, because it might embarrass the children that we'd helped. Then she added, "See, isn't it better to give than to receive?" At that time, neither my brother nor I felt any joy about the situation, but we nodded our heads anyway.

By the next day, Clint and I had forgotten about the incident and just went about the day as usual. I remember at recess I overheard one of my classmates tell the girl we'd given the clothing to that she looked very nice. You should have seen how her face lit up when she heard that. She grinned from ear to ear. My heart felt warm, and then I suddenly understood what "It's better to give than to receive" really meant.

My brother and I never told anyone about our good deed. Whenever we saw the boy and girl in their new clothes and coats we felt warm inside, knowing that our gesture had made a positive impact on their lives. That was truly the best thank you we could have gotten.

Sometimes we get so wrapped up in ourselves and in our own wants and needs that we forget to think about other people. Then, when the holidays come around, we suddenly remember that there are people in need. Try not to let giving be a "once a year" event. Even if you don't have material things to give away, you can always give your time. Volunteer at a nursing home, homeless shelter, hospital, or any other place where you can be of help to others.

7

"Dear Cassandra": Letters from Readers

"Writing letters cleanses the soul and opens the heart."

Cassandra Walker

Dear Readers,

Thank you for all of the great letters you've sent me over the past few years. You've shared your stories and problems, and asked for my help. Your letters have brought me smiles, tears, hope, and inspiration.

I know that growing up can be very difficult. I also know that your problems can sometimes overwhelm you. But you need to understand that you're not alone. Other teens have troubles like yours (I know I did!). Sometimes, realizing that you're not the only one who's struggling can make each day seem a little better.

I wanted to share some of the letters that readers have sent me, plus my responses, so you can see the real-life problems other teens are facing today. Maybe some of their problems will be similar to yours. I hope my advice has helped them and that it will help you, too.

Don't be afraid to reach out and ask for help. Talk to a parent or other relative, your teacher, a clergy member, a friend, or someone else you trust. If you want, you can write to me and I'll write back (see page 5 for the address). Keep believing in yourself and have faith, and you can get through just about anything!

Cassandra

Dear Cassandra,

My parents are constantly nagging me and giving me their advice. I don't think they understand me, and I know they don't listen to me. What can I do to get through to them, and how can I tell them to back off?

Marcus

Dear Marcus,

Many teens feel that their parents don't understand them. When you're having trouble communicating, you might be tempted to shut your parents out of your life. *Warning:* Believe it or not, parents know something about life. You might just end up learning from them!

When I was a teenager, I thought my parents knew nothing about being a teen. All of their advice seemed so outdated, and I thought they made too many rules: "Be home by midnight. . . . No phone calls after 10 PM. . . . No R-rated movies. . . ." "Get real," I thought. "I can't wait until I'm out of here." Well, the day finally came when I *was* out of there. I became an adult and had to live on my own. The funny thing was: The older I got, the smarter my parents seemed to be. Suddenly, their old rules made sense. I found out that if I stayed up late, I was tired at work the next day. When I talked on the phone all night long-distance, I ended up with an expensive phone bill and a sore throat.

From your parents' point of view, nagging is probably their way of looking out for your best interests and showing that they care. If you really listen, maybe you'll find out that your parents give good advice sometimes. Communication is a two-way street, so you need to listen to each other and understand each other's point of view. Try to talk to your parents at a time when they're not nagging you, and let them know how you feel. Good luck!

Cassandra

Dear Cassandra,

How can you tell if a boy likes you? I was wondering because this boy I know keeps teasing me. He calls me "Acne Girl" and "Skinny." What does this mean?

Denise

Dear Denise,

He probably does like you and just wants to get your attention. Some boys have a hard time showing their true feelings, so instead they throw out insults. This isn't always the case, however. Some boys who like you will find the courage to treat you with respect and kindness. Those are the ones I would open my heart to, if I were you.

Dear Cassandra,

I have very low self-esteem because of my mother. She says things like she wishes I wasn't born. She says I'm ugly, fat, and lazy. When I go to school, I hear the same things— mostly that I'm fat. It makes me feel bad, like I'm nobody. I need help, Cassandra. Please write back and give me some support and help.

Maya

Dear Maya,

First of all, you *are* somebody and never forget that.

I'm sorry to hear that your mother says those mean things to you. Unfortunately, she doesn't seem to realize how much pain she is causing you. Try talking to her about how these comments make you feel, and if that doesn't help, do your best to rise above the criticism. Find friends and family members who will love and support you. God made you, and He doesn't make junk.

Maya, if you do have a weight problem, a doctor or school nurse can tell you about safe dieting and exercise programs. A doctor can also help you to learn about nutrition and taking good care of your body. To raise your self-esteem, read books with positive messages. Also, join clubs or organizations at school or in your community so you can get together with teens who have interests similar to your own. Once people get to know you better, they'll like you for who you are and not focus so much on physical appearance. Keep your head up, because you are somebody—*somebody special.*

Cassandra

Dear Cassandra,

I have an aunt who is going to die soon because she has cancer. I am sad about this, but I am mainly worried about my mom. She had trouble with depression a few years ago, and I wonder how she is going to deal with my aunt's death. Could you please give me some advice?

Vanessa

Dear Vanessa,

I'm sorry to hear about your aunt's illness. It's very hard to lose a loved one, as I'm sure you understand.

My advice to you regarding your mother is to give her a lot of love and to support her any way that you can. She will need that from you, along with a listening ear. She may just surprise you and deal with her sister's situation better than you think she will.

My other advice to you is to take good care of yourself. This is very important when you're feeling grief from the loss of someone special. You may need to talk to a school counselor or other trusted adult during the grieving process. Or, you may find that reaching out to your mother and sharing your feelings is a good way to cope with your aunt's illness and death. Believe me, in time you and your mother will heal.

Cassandra

Dear Cassandra,

I'm starting junior high this year. I am afraid I might get lost or have a hard time adjusting. What do you suggest?

Andrew

Dear Andrew,

Starting junior high is a big deal, and you have a right to be a little apprehensive. I have a few suggestions to make your first days more enjoyable:

1. Before school starts, go visit the school. Walk around the campus, take a look at a few classrooms, and figure out where the gym, cafeteria, your locker, and other important areas are. This will help you to get acquainted with your new surroundings.

2. If the school offers an orientation, be sure to go. Take lots of notes and ask questions about the classes, rules, activities, special programs, etc.

3. Find a friend who's going to the same school, and plan to meet at different times throughout the first days to check in with each other. This will give you something to look forward to and help make the hours go by a little more quickly.

4. Remember that almost everyone will be experiencing "first-day jitters" like you. Don't worry too much about it. If you get lost or make a mistake during the day, just deal with it the best way you know how. Most importantly, try to meet new people and have a little fun!

Cassandra

Dear Cassandra,

I'm thirteen, and I want to start dating now. But my parents say I'm too young. Do you agree with them? Also, I have a friend who says her boyfriend sometimes hits her. I told her she should break up with him. What do you think?

Latoya

Dear Latoya,

First, let's talk about your friend. She's in an abusive relationship, and she needs help right away. She may think she's in love and that her boyfriend loves her, but she's in a dangerous situation.

When a boy you're dating really cares about you, he will treat you with respect and love. He will never hit you or call you cruel names. He will never treat your body in a way that you don't want him to. Try to explain this to your friend. If she doesn't take your advice and get out of the relationship, get the help of an adult you trust. Talk to a parent, teacher, counselor, or other adult who can get your friend the help she needs and keep her safe.

You asked me if I think you are too young to date. I truly feel that age sixteen is a good age to start dating (I know you may be calling me old-fashioned!). At sixteen, you are probably more mature and more ready to date. Before that, why not just be friends with boys, instead of rushing into something more serious? You'll have plenty of time in your life to date and explore new relationships, so don't be in too much of a hurry.

Cassandra

Dear Cassandra,

I have a hard time meeting people. I'm afraid they won't like me. What can I do to get better at meeting people?

Jonathan

Stories from My Life

Dear Jonathan,

Meeting new people takes courage. It's natural for you to sometimes feel shy or anxious about meeting someone new, but remember that the other person may be feeling the same way about meeting you! You must believe that you are a wonderful person and that others will be happy to know you.

To get more comfortable around strangers, be open to new experiences. Join a club, youth group, or organization that sponsors activities you enjoy. This will give you an opportunity to talk to other young people and to share your ideas and interests. At school or in your community, make new friends by introducing yourself and seeing what you have in common with others. Go to parties and dances that will encourage you to be more social. It takes practice, but soon you will overcome your fear of meeting new people.

Cassandra

Dear Cassandra,

I have a friend who I have known most of my life. We used to be very close until she started hanging around with a new group of friends. Now she wants me to be around her new friends, and all they do is curse and drink beer. I don't like their behavior, which is rubbing off on my friend. Now she is doing the same things. What can I do to save our friendship?

Angela

Dear Angela,

I understand why you would be concerned. Because this friendship is important to you, tell your friend exactly how you feel. First, let her know that you love and care about her. Then tell your friend that you're worried about her new friends and behavior. Maybe she doesn't realize that underage drinking is illegal and can be dangerous to her health. Hopefully, she'll be understanding when you talk to her.

If your friend continues to drink and curse like the other people in the group, you may have to back away from your friendship for a while. It sounds like cursing and drinking alcohol go against your values, so continue standing up for your beliefs. Make some new friends who have values similar to your own. Lastly, if you notice that your friend's behavior gets any worse, you should confide in an adult you trust. Your friend may need more help than you can give.

Cassandra

Dear Cassandra,

I am having a hard time. We moved recently. My brother is at a special school, where aids watch him every minute. I only have three friends at my new school, and people on the bus make fun of me. Can you help me?

Amanda

Stories from My Life

Dear Amanda,

Hang in there! Moving is tough enough, not to mention all the other things you're dealing with. Remember, with each move comes new opportunities. I bet that before you know it, you'll have many new friends. If not, that's okay—enjoy the friends that you do have, because they are very special.

When people tease you, stick up for yourself. You might try saying this: "Don't tease me, I don't like it." If you say this in a firm and calm voice, people will probably listen. Or, you can ignore the teasing to show that you won't let it bother you anymore. Concentrate instead on what a great person you are, and have confidence in yourself.

Lastly, maybe it's best that your brother has people watching him to see that he stays safe and has the best opportunity to learn. Give both your school and your brother's school a chance. Soon enough, you may come to realize that moving can be a positive experience.

Cassandra

Dear Cassandra,

In school, there is one boy who always makes fun of me because I have braces. Everyone else thinks that I look nice in braces. I want to believe this, but I can't believe in myself because of that boy. To tell you the truth, I think my braces make me look stupid. With this boy in my class, I can't think straight. I am so confused.

Amber

Stories from My Life

Dear Amber,

I wore braces, too! Like you, I was teased and had to learn to ignore the mean remarks. I tried to feel better about myself by making sure my hair looked nice and by always trying to look neat. But feeling good about yourself is based on more than just your appearance. Take a look at who you are *inside*. Be confident and sure about your special talents and abilities. When I finally got my braces off, I had already built up my confidence. Try it!

Cassandra

Dear Cassandra,

My face is breaking out in pimples, and people are making fun of me all the time. I can't go anywhere without people looking at me weird because of my face. I hate it when they look at me like I'm an alien. My mom took me to the dermatologist, and he gave me a cream and pills to take at bedtime. Now my face is getting much better.

I also have a learning problem that I get made fun of for. I even think of suicide sometimes because of my learning problem. Please write back.

Wayne

Dear Wayne,

Never, ever try to take your own life. You would miss your chance to grow up into that wonderful person I know you will be. If you are thinking about suicide, please talk to an adult you trust and do it today. You can reach out to your parents, a relative, a school counselor, a clergy member, a teacher, your doctor, or a social worker. Or, you can call a hotline for help. Look in your phone book under "Suicide Prevention" for hotlines staffed with people who will listen to your problems and give you the help you need. If you need to talk to someone right now and can't find a phone book, call the Boys Town National Hotline (1-800-448-3000) to reach a trained counselor who can talk to you about about crisis services.

No problem is worth taking your own life. That's why it's so important to communicate about your problems with someone you trust. Find someone to talk to whenever you're feeling down. Get a tutor to help you with your studies, and never give up on yourself. I'm glad your face is getting better—now you can heal your insides by learning to love yourself! You can do it.

Cassandra

Dear Cassandra,

I am stuck in the middle of two sisters. I love both of them, but sometimes I feel like I don't get any attention. How can I find my place?

Sharon

Dear Sharon,

You already have a place: You're an older sister to one and a younger sister to the other. Consider yourself lucky! You get the chance to give advice and be a role model to your younger sister, and at the same time, you can look up to your older sister and learn from her. You have the best of both worlds.

Instead of comparing yourself to your sisters and wondering if they are getting more attention than you, focus on yourself. Find your talent and do your best to develop it. If you like art, sports, music, writing, collecting, or some other activity, give it a try and polish your skills. You'll see that the best way to feel happy is by doing your own thing.

Cassandra

Dear Cassandra,

I think I am fat. I don't like it when others call me "Chubby." I want to look pretty like the women I see on television and in the magazines. I feel depressed when I see them and then look at myself.

Eliza

Dear Eliza,

Many teen girls (and boys) worry about their appearance. I can totally understand how pressured you feel to look like a model because TV, movies, and magazines tell us that's the way to look. But you must remember that no one is perfect. People on TV and in magazines have make-up artists and hairstylists helping them to look beautiful.

Many young people going through puberty find that all the changes in their bodies are hard to deal with. But this is all perfectly normal! Don't compare yourself to the impossible standards set by TV and magazines, and don't listen to people who say you're chubby. If you eat right, exercise, and get the rest you need, your body will develop into a wonderful creation.

What counts most is what's on the inside (no matter how many times you've heard that, it still remains true!). I was a skinny girl with large lips and no hips, and today I have no problems meeting new people and feeling good about myself. I wish I hadn't worried so much about my appearance when I was growing up!

Cassandra

Dear Cassandra,

What is your suggestion for finding a part-time job that is right for me? I can't seem to find one that I really like, so I keep quitting.

Carl

Dear Carl,

Many teens get after-school jobs to help support their families, save up for college, or make a little extra spending money. Having a job not only provides a source of income but also a learning experience. A job can teach you skills that will last a lifetime.

Try to figure out what has been frustrating about the jobs you've had. Did you have problems with the hours, the duties, your boss, your coworkers? Is there something else you could have done to improve the situation, rather than quitting? Quitting isn't always the best option; it may be your way of not facing what's really on your mind.

To determine what kind of job is right for you, think about what you're interested in and good at. If you love animals, try to get a job at an animal shelter or pet shop. If you dream of being a writer, find out what opportunities exist for young people at a local newspaper or publishing company. Your school or community may have a job-placement program that could help you pinpoint your interests and find employment. We had a program like that when I was in school, and it was very helpful.

Cassandra

Dear Cassandra,

My parents aren't very supportive, and they don't give me much encouragement. Whenever I try something new, they say things like, "Are you sure you can do that?" I pretend it doesn't bug me, but things like that build up after a while.

The most recent thing has been that I want to be a lifeguard this summer. When I told my mother, she put me down and said she wasn't sure I could do it.

Tricia

Dear Tricia,

It's hard when we don't have the support of our parents, but it doesn't make us less capable. Find other sources of support: friends, teachers, mentors, relatives, etc. Even if no one is backing you up, you can still do your best and achieve.

Try to tell your parents how you really feel about their comments. It may help your mom and dad to understand you better. Remember, if they still don't support you, find the courage to support yourself, and GO FOR IT! One day, they will probably say: "Hey, we're proud of you!" I know I'm proud of you.

Cassandra

Dear Cassandra,

I have a problem saying no to people who ask me to do things for them. Whenever someone asks me to do some homework for them, or go here or there, I say "Okay," even when it is inconvenient for me. I want to keep my friends and be popular. I need to learn to say NO!

Mary

Dear Mary,

Being popular is very important to many teens. Some teenagers will do anything to gain popularity, even if they lose themselves in the process. Don't sacrifice your own happiness to please others. Be confident in yourself and your own needs, then learn to communicate more effectively. Next time you find yourself in a situation where you are tempted to say yes, even though you really want to say no, try this:

1. Ask yourself: Can I really do this? Do I really *want* to?
2. If you decide that no is your answer, then admit it to yourself and to the other person. Firmly and politely tell the person no by saying, "I can't at this time," or "I'm sorry, but I'm not interested in doing that."

Once you get the hang of saying no, it will get easier. Most importantly, never be afraid to say no if you are asked to compromise your own beliefs or standards. If that happens, don't hesitate—say it loud and clear: NO!! You'll be on your way to saying yes to a better life!

Cassandra

About the Author

assandra Walker, a popular speaker and syndicated columnist, received her B.A. in Mass Communications from Western Illinois University. She worked as a newspaper reporter, public relations director, English teacher, and public speaker before moving to radio and television. Cassandra was a former youth reporter and host of "Youth Corner" for WCCO TV in Minneapolis, Minnesota. She is the author of *Becoming Myself: True Stories about Learning from Life*.

Today, Cassandra enjoys taking care of her family, writing, and public speaking. Her newspaper column, "Sharing," incorporates story-telling techniques to offer guidance to teens who have questions about life issues. The column has been turned into a weekly radio segment. Cassandra was recently honored as a 1997 Black Woman of Distinction for Kansas City, Kansas, and the greater-metropolitan area.

To order or request a free catalog, please contact:

Free Spirit Publishing, Inc.
400 First Avenue North, Suite 616
Minneapolis, MN 55401-1730
1-800-735-7323
(612) 338-2068
help4kids@freespirit.com